DISCIPLESHIP

FOR CATHOLIC MEN

NFCM

NATIONAL FELLOWSHIP OF CATHOLIC MEN

Embracing God's
Plan for Our Life

National Fellowship of Catholic Men

301-474-1043   info@nfcmusa.org
www.catholicmensresources.org

"Catholic men, Linked as Brothers in Jesus Christ, and Called to Bring Him to Others"

NFCM

NATIONAL FELLOWSHIP OF CATHOLIC MEN

GOD IS MOVING IN HEARTS OF CATHOLIC MEN ALL ACROSS THE U.S.:

➤ 40 Catholic Men's Conferences were conducted in 2006.
➤ Over 45 conferences planned for 2007.
➤ Thousands of parish-based Catholic men's fellowship groups established.

OUR GOAL

➤ Help bring Catholic men's conferences to all parts of the US
➤ Support men's fellowship groups in all 19,000 US Parishes.
➤ Provide high-quality Catholic small group and leadership resources for Catholic men and fellowship groups.

THE RESULT

Enrich your life and your faith, individually, and as part of a Catholic men's fellowship group.

COME AND SEE

Go to www.catholicmensresources.org for Catholic men's resources, Sunday Mass Readings and meditations with discussion questions, Catholic men's e-zine, CD of the Month Club, forums, and much more.

ALL PHOTOGRAPHS AND LINE ART IS EITHER THE WORK OF THE AUTHOR OR IN THE PUBLIC DOMAIN.

THE Scripture PASSAGES CONTAINED HEREIN ARE FROM THE REVISED STANDARD VERSION BIBLE, COPYRIGHT © 1952, 1971, BY THE DIVISION OF CHRISTIAN EDUCATION OF THE NATIONAL COUNCIL OF CHURCHES OF CHRIST IN THE UNITED STATES OF AMERICA. ALL RIGHTS RESERVED.

Excerpts from the English translation of the Catechism of the Catholic Church for the United States of America © 1994, United States Catholic Conference, Inc. Libreria Editrice Vaticana. Cited in the text as "CCC."

PARISH LIFE SERVICES PRESS
850 WATERSHED DR.
Ann Arbor, MI 48105
www.ParishLifeServices.org
ISBN: 978-1-4243-4239-6

Copyright © 2007 Parish Life Services. All rights reserved.

Printed in the United States of America

TABLE OF CONTENTS

Foreword by Maurice Blumberg

Executive Director, National Fellowship of Catholic Men

This is truly an exciting time to follow the Lord Jesus Christ! There is no more fulfilling and joyful life than that of being a disciple of Jesus Christ. The *Catechism of the Catholic Church* defines the life of a disciple this way: "The disciple of Christ must not only keep the faith and live on it, but also profess it, confidently bear witness to it, and spread it" (1816).

We believe that the Lord is calling men in the Catholic men's movement to focus more on *discipleship*. Discipleship may have an unfamiliar ring for many Catholics. What does discipleship mean? In a word, from the scriptural accounts of how Jesus and Paul discipled as well as the many examples of saints, we see, above all, that we follow a person, rather than merely assent to religious truth or try to adhere to a certain morality. Hence, discipleship begins and ends with the Lord Jesus Christ, with personally encountering the Lord in prayer, scripture reading, the sacraments, and even in relationships with other men.

Discipleship, then, turns on having a relationship with a *master*, none other than God himself in the person of Jesus. Our relationship is characterized by "belonging" to God and by obedience to him. Part I of *Discipleship for Catholic Men* rightly identifies one of the pivotal steps in becoming a disciple: making Jesus "Lord of Our Life", that is, to give our lives (back) to God and pledge obedience to following his will. In many cases, making Jesus Lord is the missing step in conversion.

In the *Mission of the Redeemer*, Pope John Paul II tied conversion to being a disciple in this way: "Conversion means accepting, by a personal decision, the saving sovereignty of Christ and becoming his disciple."

If we fundamentally commit ourselves to Jesus as disciples by making him Lord, the battle for holiness and obtaining a life of charity is half won. Part II of *Discipleship for Catholic* men first takes up some of the challenges to being a disciple and then considers some of the specific ways in which we must be obedient to our Lord. Conversion, transformation and mobilization for mission are the stages of spiritual growth that helps us unpack God's plan for us as his disciples.

The time has come for the Catholic men's movement – indeed, for the entire Church – to becoming thoroughly grounded in discipleship. God is calling all of us to a deep conversion, a glorious transformation, and a mission that befits his sons (and daughters). The strange irony of the Christian life is that the more completely we give ourselves up to, and embrace, God's plan for our life – even though it might require great effort and sacrifice – the more joyful, happy, and fulfilled we become. But, then, as the Lord himself says, he came and suffered for us in order that our joy might be complete! (John 15.11)

Introduction

Are you looking for joy, true joy? Not simply the flush of success, a wave of pleasure, or the quiet of a serene and beautiful place? Nor simply the passing elation of achievement, the fleetingness of sensible delight, or a temporary abatement from the stresses of life? All of us look for true joy unless, in frustration, we deny its existence. In fact, God *made you* for joy and *longs for you* to embrace it. The source of this joy is a relationship with God through Jesus Christ.

Discipleship *is* embracing God's plan for our lives; it is sometimes referred to as *spiritual formation*. God has a general plan for everyone, but also a unique design for each of us. As plans for any house call for foundations, walls, doors, windows and a roof but may vary greatly as to size, layout, and building materials, so God's plan for you has both common and unique features. The common features include:

1. being with God and his people;
2. becoming like Jesus; and
3. loving whom and what God loves.

As God is the master-builder of our lives, he not only has the plan but also does the work! While we must embrace God's plan, he eagerly provides the grace and power to be with him, become like him and love those whom he loves.

(AP Photo/Nick Wass)

Structure of Book. Part I of *Discipleship for Catholic Men* identifies God's call of discipleship to all Catholic men in six lessons, while Part II is comprised of thirty-two lessons on the basics of discipleship. Most lessons feature relevant passages from Scripture and the *Catechism of the Catholic Church ("CCC")* which the reader investigates in the fashion of a traditional bible study. Each lesson also includes application exercises, discussion questions, or both. *Discipleship for Catholic Men* is essentially a handbook on the basics of discipleship, to be studied as a workbook. For sake of simplicity and ease of further study, references are generally limited to *Sacred Scripture* and the *CCC*.

Use of this Book. *Discipleship for Catholic Men* is designed to be used by two or more men meeting regularly for about one hour to review and discuss each lesson. The meeting format and dynamics are summarized in "Suggestions for Group Study" at the end of this book, and discussed in Part I, Lesson 6 and in an Appendix. The thirty-eight lesson may be covered in nine months to one and one half years, depending on whether the group meets weekly or bi-weekly. Ideally, each participant will invest at least one-half hour preparing each lesson. Since it is often difficult to read and prepare ahead of time, sections of each lesson should be read out loud and time allowed for individuals to complete the exercises and lessons. Discussion group leader guides are downloadable for free from www.GodsPlanforYourLife.org. Of course, one could study the book with profit on their own. Recommendations for further study may be found in Lesson 32 of Part II.

Part I Discipleship: God's Call to Catholic Men

"COME, FOLLOW ME"

1 - Discipleship Is Following God's Plan for Our Life

> *4**He chose us** in him before the foundation of the world to be holy and blameless before him in love. 5**He destined us** for adoption as his children through Jesus Christ, according to the good pleasure of his will, . . . 10**as a plan for the fullness of time**, to unite all things in him, things in heaven and things on earth.*
>
> Ephesians 1

Jesus invited the first disciples to "come, follow me." These disciples literally left what they were doing – whether fishing, tax collecting or lawyering – and went to follow Jesus. Where are we at? What have we filled our lives with – and why? If Jesus calls us to follow him, what's his plan?

The notion of discipleship implies a change as we abandon our own plans – probably deeply influenced by society - and follow Jesus' plan. Jesus forms our life anew – not just "spiritually" but also in a very concrete and practical manner. <u>Disciples of the Lord Jesus should, and will, look different than people formed in a worldly way.</u> This lesson considers how the world forms us and the plan we have for our life, while the next lesson introduces the three main components of God's plan for us.

The World's Plans

American culture brims with plans for every facet of our life, starting with when, if and how you are made. Public schools educate and instill "values"; the media and video games decimate your attention span. Take Big Gulps then let Atkins shed your fat. Soft porn TV shows; hard porn only clicks away. If it *feels good*, do it! Big toys for big boys. Consume your way to happiness, then let a lawyer shred your credit card debt. Give your all to get ahead, but no hard feelings if you get canned. *You're entitled to a good life!* Kids' activities first, second and third, even as your marriage falls apart. Just find what you are really good at, and do it. Smarts, hard work, and good looks. Stay connected. Multi-task. Quality time with the family *over a TV dinner*. Work hard, play hard. Just do it: you are *what you do*. The main thing is that you try to be nice and that you feel good about yourself – it's all in your head. You just need some anger management. Therapy and pills. It's OK, as long as you aren't hurting anybody. *Don't Worry, Be Happy*. Indeed, our culture and society has suggestions and plans for who we are, what will make us happy, our purpose in life, how to relate to other people, what to value, how to shape the basic patterns of our day, and how to make major life choices. Catholics are hardly immune to cultural suggestions on what to do and who to be.

How many guys plan their weekends around watching football games or other sporting activities? How many begin Saturday morning with a time of prayer, bible study, or Mass, even at the expense of watching only part of the football game or playing nine holes instead of eighteen? Unless we deliberately choose how to approach our leisure time, work, marriage, child rearing, etc., we probably adopt the world's approach by default. Consider some of the plans or ideas that American culture has for us. List several worldly approaches for the following areas:

Pleasures
> *Instant gratification*
> _____

Being Successful
> *Status & money are everything*
> _____

The Perfect Spouse
> *Gives you independence*
> _____

Personal Appearance
> *Clothes are very important*
> *I am how I appear*

Getting Ahead
> *Whatever it takes*
> _____

The Perfect Child
> *Your friend*
> *makes own decisions*

Free Time or Leisure
> *All about me*
> *Drinking & partying hard*

> **The Meaning of Life**
>
> Jesus lays out the meaning of life (and of his death) in chapters 15-17 of John's gospel; see especially 15.11 and 16.20-24. What is the basis for this joy?
> _____
> _____
> _____
> _____

Identity –
child of God
vs.

So, What About Your Plans?

What did you think would make you happy in life back in your high school days?

_____

_____

What is your purpose in life? Do you have two or three overall objectives for your life?

_____

_____

Power of Spirit   *Google Doc*

List several things you do on a typical summer weekend. What got you started doing them?

Activity   How you started/Why you keep doing it

_____

_____

_____

_____

What are some of your long-term plans for work (or retirement)? What are your overall goals?

_____

_____

_____

_____

Where Do the World's Plans Take Us?

Doubtless your life is fairly unique, reflecting not only your own drives and choices, but also the influence of our culture and society. Chances are your life is not exactly perfect. The following harsh statistics apply even to those attending church regularly. According to Patrick Morley (author of *Man in the Mirror*), for every 10 men,

- 9 will have kids who leave the church
- 8 will not find their jobs satisfying
- 6 pay the monthly minimum on their credit cards
- 5 have a major problem with pornography
- 4 will get divorced
- All 10 will struggle to balance work and family

Most of us are, in fact, deeply influenced by our culture, and many of us experience the problems listed above or are otherwise unhappy. As many of us know, the world's plans yield little long-term happiness. Scripture speaks of

> ### Rich Man, Poor Man
>
> I was dazzled by the possibilities opening up to me. I could be fabulously rich – I knew it. I had just finished the novel *Rich Man, Poor Man* by Irwin Shaw when I was in about ninth grade. Somehow I took away from the book that I could accomplish anything I set my heart to, a notion my parents also emphasized. What was I going to be when I grew up? *Successful.* Success became the overriding objective in my life.

the "world" as the negative moral and spiritual influence that society and culture[a] exerts. What are the forces behind it? Capitalism, especially advertising, and democracy, with its emphasis on individual rights and freedoms, are some of the major factors driving American society and culture. Catholics believe that another significant force is at work in our culture, which explicitly strives to undermine God's plans for our lives:

---

[a] *Society* is a community, nation, or broad grouping of people having common traditions, institutions, and collective activities and interests and *culture* is the totality of socially transmitted behavior patterns, arts, beliefs, institutions, and all other products of human work and thought. Merriam-Webster's *Dictionary of Law*, © 1996 and *The American Heritage® Dictionary of the English Language*, Fourth Edition, respectively, downloaded from Dictionary.com in May, 2005.

Satan or the devil and the other demons are fallen angels who have freely refused to serve God and his plan. Their choice against God is definitive. They try to associate man in their revolt against God. (CCC 414)

More on the "world" in Part II; suffice it to note here that much that the world offers is illusory and fails to provide deep, long-lasting joy.

Have Your Plans Made You Happy?

At the end of the day, the ultimate measure of any plan is how happy or joyful it makes you. Since everybody instinctively tries to "look happy," joy may be the better descriptor. It's hard to fake joy. Joy is deep and abiding, rather than some manufactured emotional state. Most of us probably never stop to think much about joy. Pleasure, sex, victory, accomplishment, success, fun, athletic glory – yes. JOY – no, unless you're a bit strange. Joy or deep abiding happiness is really what life's all about.

Widner/NBA via Getty

The elation of nailing the game-winner is a crude sort of "joy," usually bordering on personal glory. It's joy – but it quickly passes, at least by the inevitable next defeat. And how many people actually hit the game-winner? *What produces true joy which never fades or grows boring, even after a thousand years?* We long for such joy. Indeed, we were made for such joy.

God's Plan Brings Us Eternal Joy

Thanks be to God that Jesus has a plan that makes us eternally happy and joyful! Out of his immense love for us he desires and makes it possible to "be all that we can be." Unlike joining the Army, Jesus' plan transforms us to be little less than God (Ps 8) and prepares us to enjoy the eternal riches prepared for us (Matthew 25:34), yielding true and eternal joy (Matthew 25.21; John 15.11); in the words of St. Peter, an indescribable and glorious joy (I Peter 1.8).

Discussion Question #1. How would you describe God's plan for your life?
Lead family to heaven
_____
_____

Discussion Question #2. How does God's plan impact your daily life? List some specifics.
How spend time, talent, treasure
_____
_____

Lesson 2 - A Roadmap for Implementing God's Plan for Your Life

All things were created through him and for him.   Colossians 1.16

God made us with very specific ends in mind. And he made us in such a way that when we pursue these objectives, we find great joy. Seeking deep happiness or joy is something like a "homing" instinct that pushes and guides us towards God. Following God's plan for our life yields the truest and deepest joy, and this plan has three major elements: being with him and his people, becoming like him, and loving whom he loves.

Although God tailors his plan to exactly who we are, these basic goals are the same for every human being. First, he made us in order to have a relationship with us. Go no further – this is the purpose of our life. This is why God made us free. This is why he made us the greatest kind of creature; God made us just like himself, in his image. God may have a *gerbil* for a pet but he wants *us* as a member of his family. So **being with God** also puts us in a brother and sister relationship with all his other sons and daughters.

He made us like himself so that he could have the best possible kind of persons in his family. Hmmm. Stop to think about it and one notices that even on a good day, most of us little resemble God, at least as revealed in the person of Jesus. I'm not sure that I would want to be in a family for all eternity made up of people like myself, at least such as I am today. The second overall goal in God's plan for us, in fact, is to **make us become like Jesus**.

As God helps us become like Jesus, not only do our characters come to resemble Jesus in holiness, attractiveness, kindness, lovingness, lovability, and so on, but what we love and the things for which we work naturally become what God loves and those things for which God works. **Loving whom God loves** is the third goal in his plan for us.

These three goals – or peaks, if you will – in a certain way define our life's quest. The imagery of scaling peaks implies, perhaps, one-sided effort on our part. Our effort in many ways, however, is more akin to climbing aboard God's Jeep and having the good sense to stay put. We will consider God's role and our efforts in more detail later in the section on *Equipping for Battle*. The rest of this lesson will introduce the spiritual processes through which God works out his plan in our lives. The following two lessons then consider the possibility of a men's group assisting with this spiritual growth, while Part I closes with a lesson challenging us to make a crucial first step in our life of discipleship.

Discussion Question #1. Do you believe that following God's plan for your life will make you happy? Why or why not?

_____

_____

_____

Embracing God's Plan for Our Life

The general goals of God's plan for our life are to be with him, to become like him and to love whom he loves. How does God use his Holy Spirit, Scripture, the Church, the sacraments, the lives of the saints, our small group, and other tools to bring this about? God's work of implementing his plan for our life can be broken down into three spiritual processes:

Be With Him

Conversion

Transformation   MISSION

Become Like Him

Love Who He Loves

Conversion	God brings us into a relationship with himself and his people when we repent and accept forgiveness and make Jesus Lord.
Transformation	God makes us like Jesus, in terms of holiness and being filling us with his empowering Spirit.
Embracing Mission	God infuses us with his Power to love others by caring for their needs, evangelizing them to Christ, and serving within the Church.

As Catholics, we understand that in a certain sense our "conversion" is lifelong: we need to keep repenting and keep going to confession. We often neglect a crucial key to having a relationship with God, namely, recognizing his lordship and sovereignty in our lives and living this out on a daily basis. The rest of this lesson summarizes conversion. Personal prayer and the sacraments are at the heart of conversion, transformation and embracing mission; the scope of this book is limited to covering only personal prayer, (see "Basic Training," Part II). Transformation and embracing mission, are considered in the balance of Part II.

Conversion Brings Us into Life with God and His People

This study pre-supposes that you have a basic understanding of conversion and that you are sacramentally participating in the life of grace and the life of the Church. By way of refresher, the following diagram is one way to illustrate the steps related to conversion:

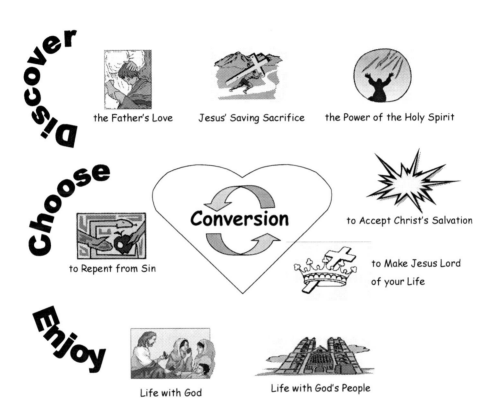

Discover the Father's Love • Jesus' Saving Sacrifice • the Power of the Holy Spirit

Conversion

to Accept Christ's Salvation

to Make Jesus Lord of your Life

Choose to Repent from Sin

Enjoy Life with God • Life with God's People

Our heavenly father knows exactly who we are and loves each of us deeply – he crafted us uniquely in our mother's womb, he has counted every hair of our heads and knows when we sit and when we stand (Ps 139; Lk 12.6-7). He loves us so much that he sent his son to make up for the damage done by our sins by suffering on the cross (Jn 3.16-17); even when we fail badly, he is ready to welcome us home (Lk 15.11-32). God only requires that we repent (turn away) from our sins and accept salvation – new life – through the saving sacrifice of Jesus. In becoming followers of Jesus, we give our lives to him definitively: we are no longer our own (I Cor 6.19) and Jesus is our Lord (Rom 14.7-8). In the words of a holy saint, we give what we do not own in order to gain what we cannot lose. What we gain – a truly indescribable intimacy and personal relationship with God and his people – is the only true source of joy.

The archetypical conversion story is that of the Apostle Paul. Read Acts 26.9-18 and paraphrase verse 18 in your own words.

_____

_____

_____

_____

_____

Discussion Question #2. In what ways have you experienced God's love as your father? How have your experiences with your natural father helped or hindered your experience of God's love?

_____

_____

_____

Discussion Question #3. What area of conversion do you struggle with most – repenting, asking forgiveness, or making Jesus lord of your life? Why?

_____

_____

_____

Above we touched on the crucial first step of a disciple: making Jesus lord of our life. After considering in the next two lessons how Jesus' first disciple's made him lord of their lives, how Jesus discipled them as a Men's Group, and how he wishes to disciple us today, we will return to how we tangibly and concretely make Jesus Lord of our lives in the concluding section of Part I.

Lesson 3 - Being a 1st Century Disciple in Jesus' Men's Group

Imagine life as one of Jesus' first disciples. Entering into a master-disciple relationship, we move with him throughout Galilee and back and forth to Jerusalem. As a member of a group numbering less than twenty or thirty, Jesus gets to know us quite well. Read the following passages from the beginning of Mark's gospel:

> 1.16 And passing along by the Sea of Galilee, he saw Simon and Andrew the brother of Simon casting a net in the sea; for they were fishermen. 17 And Jesus said to them, "Follow me and I will make you become fishers of men." 18 And immediately they left their nets and followed him. 19 And going on a little farther, he saw James the son of Zebedee and John his brother, who were in their boat mending the nets. 20 And immediately he called them; and they left their father Zebedee in the boat with the hired servants, and followed him . . . 1.38 And he said to them, "Let us go on to the next towns, that I may preach there also; for that is why I came out." 39 And he went throughout all Galilee, preaching in their synagogues and casting out demons.
>
> 3.13 And he went up on the mountain, and called to him those whom he desired; and they came to him. 14 And he appointed twelve, to be with him, and to be sent out to preach . . . 3.32 And a crowd was sitting about him; and they said to him, "Your mother and your brothers are outside, asking for you." 33 And he replied, "Who are my mother and my brothers?" 34 And looking around on those who sat about him, he said, "Here are my mother and my brothers! 35 Whoever does the will of God is my brother, and sister, and mother."

What do you suppose would be the best part about getting to know Jesus so intimately? What would be the scariest?

_____

_____

_____

_____

Life with God, Up Close and Personal

Experiencing Jesus' tremendous love and goodness reveals what life with God is like: knowing Jesus is knowing the Father. And this is the defining relationship of our life, one that comes before all others. Read John 14.7-11. Why do you think it was so difficult for Thomas and Philip to recognize the Father in Jesus?

_____

_____

_____

_____

What kind of advantage did Peter, James and John enjoy in this regard, as described in Matthew 17.1-6?

_____

_____

_____

_____

Being so close to Jesus over a three year period forces us to measure ourselves against Jesus' character and holiness, his warmth and love, and the quality of his friendship towards us. His example of how to be human, what to do and for what to live is irresistible. Jesus' perfection and goodness reveals one's cheapness and poverty of life; one either flees his presence or pleads for his help to become like him!

Absolute Obedience

As our master, he challenges, critiques and disciplines us. Jesus means business and requires absolute obedience. While free to sever the master-disciple relationship at any time, we want Jesus' help no matter what the cost. Indeed, his lordship has teeth.

> *So therefore, whoever of you does not renounce all that he has cannot be my disciple.*   Luke 14:33

Take some time to consider the meaning of these words and those found in Matthew 7.13-28. How would you feel about someone asserting that kind of authority over you?

_____

_____

_____

_____

Radical Transformation

Read Matthew 5. A challenging call, but we would know that Jesus is committed to seeing us through to the goal of becoming perfect like your heavenly father (verse 48), as our master but also sympathetic and encouraging. Jesus' first disciples meet the radical call to holiness of the Sermon on the Mount (Matthew 5) only by surrendering themselves completely to his lordship.

What do you think Jesus means by his saying in Matthew 11.28-30?

_____

_____

_____

_____

Your master's absolute commitment to transforming us, however difficult the task, with a gentle firmness is enormously encouraging. Anything less from Jesus and we would give up before we got started. The power radiating from him converts our intentions into concrete changes in our lives. By the end of a few years, we grow very much like Jesus, coming to be filled with the Holy Spirit.

Whether members of that first group or trying to be a disciple today, Jesus provides the power both to be like him and to love other people. What is the key to receiving this power in John 15.5-10?

_____

_____

_____

_____

What is one tangible way of drawing close to Jesus as disciples living today, described in John 6.41-58?

_____

_____

_____

_____

Filled with the Holy Spirit

Again, picturing ourselves as one of Jesus' first disciples, the work of our master would have become our work, his priorities our priorities, his loves our loves, his joys our joys. We would see things through his eyes, we would think as he thought, yet not as some kind of slave but as a friend and co-worker. Rather than be subsumed by his personality and agenda, we would joyfully emerge more ourselves than we could ever imagine. The deepest contours of our personality, perhaps deformed and corrupted from prior ill

---

Smell Good?

14 But thanks be to God, who in Christ always leads us in triumph, and through us spreads the fragrance of the knowledge of him everywhere. 15 For we are the aroma of Christ to God among those who are being saved and among those who are perishing, 16 to one a fragrance from death to death, to the other a fragrance from life to life.

II Corinthians 2:14-16

use, are re-made and brought forth in splendor. Yet whatever radiance we have is in proportion to how fully we participate in the life of God and are filled with his grace and power. Indeed, dozens if not hundreds or thousands would see our example and hear our preaching and would want to be like us, gain what we have gained, as was the case with the Apostles as they fanned out from Jerusalem carrying on the Lord Jesus' work.

Read Acts 2.1-21, 37-41. What is the key to Peter's preaching that converts 3,000 in one day?

_____

_____

_____

_____

_____

The Holy Spirit plays a big role in, well, EVERYTHING. So, throughout this book we'll constantly consider the role of the Holy Spirit, *aka* God's Grace, in how we can grow as disciples. The next lesson considers how Jesus wants to disciple us, in part, through our men's group.

Lesson 4 - Being a 21st Century Disciple in a Men's Group

Although Jesus surely taught his disciples individually, the gospel records indicate that he primarily formed them as disciples in the context of his men's group. Does Jesus wish to form us as disciples today? Can our men's group serve this purpose well? How can he be present to our men's group to disciple us?

First Disciples Better Off without Him? (trick question)

Jesus says some rather strange things to his Men's Group on the night of his arrest:

> Yet a little while, and the world will see me no more, but you will see me; because I live, you will live also. In that day you will know that I am in my Father, and you in me, and I in you . . . it is to your advantage that I go away, for if I do not go away, the Counselor will not come to you; but if I go, I will send him to you. (John 14.19-20, 16.7)

Could it be that his disciples were better off without Jesus physically present to them? Jesus seems to say so. Why? Because Jesus sends his Spirit only after his departure. In fact, throughout Jesus' last discourse with his men's group he emphasizes the amazing intimacy he will have with them *only after he departs!* (John 14-17)

Read John 15.1-17. Describe the keys for Jesus' Men's Group to dwell with or abide with Jesus after his departure.

_____
_____
_____
_____

In what ways do you suppose Jesus expected his Men's Group to continue loving one another after his departure?

_____
_____
_____
_____

How do you suppose Jesus wishes to be present to your men's group (see also Matthew 18.20 and 28.20)?

_____

_____

_____

_____

Jesus' Wants to Disciple YOU!

Jesus promised his powerful ongoing presence to the group of men he discipled, and he extends this promise to your men's group to the extent you and your group follow Jesus' commands and ask him to be present through prayer. But does he want to disciple us?

What were the final marching orders that Jesus gave his men's group in Matthew 28.19-20? Do you think the Lord wants to apply these instructions to your men's group? How?

_____

_____

_____

_____

_____

Not only does Jesus instruct his initial men's group to make disciples, but Christians down to the present age have taken this final command of Jesus with the utmost seriousness. Consider the typically strong emphasis on the necessity of discipleship, or spiritual formation, found in John Paul II's Apostolic Letter "On the Christian Laity"[1]:

> People are approached in liberty by God who calls everyone to grow, develop and bear fruit . . . [to the] necessity of a total and ongoing formation . . . a continual process in the individual of maturation in faith and a likening to Christ, according to the will of the Father, under the guidance of the Holy Spirit . . . spiritual formation ought to occupy a privileged place in a person's life. Everyone is called to grow continually in intimate union with Jesus Christ, in conformity to the Father's will, in devotion to others in charity and justice.

Ways and Means

So how does God intend to disciple all of us who missed being a part of Jesus' first men's group? How might God bring about his plan for our lives? After all, as it was for the first disciples, achieving God's plan for our lives is inconceivable without his help and power. Fortunately, he has the following instruments at his disposal:

Tool	*Application*
Sacred Scripture	Jesus reveals himself and what life as sons of God is like and provides a program for transforming our lives into becoming like him.
the Holy Spirit	Through this gift, Jesus allows us to be with God even now and provides the power to help us become like him and to do the work he does.
the Church	Jesus incorporates us into his very own body, through which he nourishes us, forgiving our sins and allowing us to participate in the power of his resurrection in the Mass, and in which we enjoy life with his people.
the Lives of the Saints	Jesus provides men (and women), both through the ages and living today, who exemplify the fullness of living with God, becoming like him and living for his purposes. Saints are both models and inspiration.

Some Catholics are also privileged to enjoy a *Spiritual Mentor or Director*. A spiritual mentor or director assists the work of God in an individual's life by helping a person employ the tools above with human wisdom and by modeling in their own person, to some degree, how to embrace God's plan for our life. Relatively few spiritual directors are available for the millions of practicing Catholics in this country. Some Catholics, however, have received, to some degree, spiritual direction from their parents.

Many Catholics could use a great deal of help in understanding and adopting God's plan for their lives. Many come from less than perfect families that gave little heed to God's plan, and few have the benefit of a hands-on spiritual director or mentor. Today, the Church recognizes that additional help is needed with implementing God's plan for our lives:

> Small communities [*such as men's groups*] are powerful vehicles for adult faith formation, providing opportunities for learning, prayer, mutual support, and shared experience of Christian living and service to Church and society. Ecclesial movements and associations [*such as the National Fellowship of Catholic Men*] that are part of the vibrant life of the Church make great contributions here. We welcome this phenomenon as "a sign of the Church's vitality." [2]

In fact, the best model for spiritual growth may be the first: joining a group of men who wish to be discipled by Jesus. While Jesus won't be present as a man, he does promise to be with two or more disciples when they gather in his name through the Holy Spirit. Employing Scripture and Church Teaching, Jesus can be present though the Holy Spirit to disciple us and help bring about God's plan for our life. Many of us already participate in a men's group. This study is intended to provide a vision for, and assist in implementing, a program that will allow God to use your men's group to advance his plans for your lives.

> ### My First Men's Group
>
> My men's group leader was challenging us to be *radical for Christ*. I have to say I jumped at this challenge at the idealist age of eighteen much more than I might now. As a freshman in college, I was shooting for the stars – as a newly serious Catholic, I wanted to be not just any disciple, but a radical disciple. I suppose it's not for nothing that I am named Peter, experiencing both heightened zeal and sorry failures as a disciple.
>
> Two of the other four guys in my group seemed a little weird – one clearly a nerd, the other a bit too self-confident. Still, I knew they loved Christ. I remember one perceiving my attraction to a particular co-ed and cautioning me to be careful in expressing my affection – just the encouragement I needed at the time.
>
> God really worked through our praying together, discussing Scripture together, caring for one another, and studying together. I owe a significant amount of my formation as a disciple to that group.

The Vision Thing

Up to this point, how would you describe the purpose of your men's group?

_____
_____
_____
_____

What kind of vision do you have now for God using your men's group as a help in being with him, growing more like him, and loving whom he loves?

_____
_____
_____
_____

But let's not put the cart before the horse. Jesus can only work through our men's group if each of us individually makes Jesus Lord of our life – which is the subject of the next lesson. We will then begin the next part of this book with broadening the vision for our men's group to include discipleship.

Lesson 5 – Making Jesus Lord of Your Life

God has highly exalted him and bestowed on him the name which is above every name, that at the name of Jesus every knee should bow, in heaven and on earth and under the earth, and every tongue confess that Jesus Christ is Lord, to the glory of God the Father.   Philippians 2.9-11

The crucial first step of discipleship – after repentance and seeking God's forgiveness in Christ – is to decide definitively to give your entire life to Jesus and to follow both his general commands and his specific instructions to you in anything and everything. Giving everything and obeying in all things are the two fundamental aspects of making Jesus lord of our life. No wonder that the New Testament word for conversion, *metanoia*, describes a complete and definitive change of life.

As we saw in Lesson 3, the change God has in mind for us as disciples is to such complete holiness and love for others that we must surrender ourselves fully to Jesus' lordship. Jesus can then transform us into creatures who naturally find our highest joy in loving him and his people, as he pours God's love into our hearts through the Holy Spirit (Romans 5.5). This transformation depends upon us saying "yes" to Jesus, opening our hearts to him, and fully entrusting him with our lives. Our permission essentially amounts to following his direction, being with him, and drawing on the power he so graciously and abundantly provides.

The Lordship of Christ: Belonging to God

You are not your own; you were bought with a price.   I Corinthians 6.19

We belong to God in two fundamental ways. As our creator, we belong to him as his creatures, in a certain sense, despite possessing free will. We were created in order to have a relationship with God and his people, one providing indescribable joy. Sin abuses our free will by destroying ourselves and others, and so renders us unfit for a relationship with God and others. Without God intervening by paying the price to make up or "atone for" the damage of our sins by dying on the cross, we would face death and dissolution – and so the saying in I Corinthians that heads this section. Since Jesus redeems us from death, we belong to God in this second way. By making Jesus lord of our lives, we recognize his ownership of our lives. What does God have in mind for these "possessions" he purchased, as it were, by the blood of the cross? To make us capable of enjoying his fantastic company and that of all others who are so transformed. And so transformed, we are possessed by the same love God has for other people (II Corinthians 5.14).

Application Question #1 – Read Mark 8.34-37. How would you describe the level of conviction you must have in order to literally follow these words of Jesus?

_____

_____

_____

The Lordship of Christ: Obedience

Not every one who says to me, 'Lord, Lord,' shall enter the kingdom of heaven, but he who does the will of my Father who is in heaven.   Matthew 7.21

The will of our heavenly Father is expressed preeminently in Scripture, particularly in the teaching of his son, Jesus, and through the ongoing leading and direction of the Holy Spirit in our lives, and through the teaching office of the Church. Obedience is the second aspect of Jesus' lordship of our lives. Our obedience allows God to transform us. Of course, obedience takes trust in God and his intentions for our life. Adam doubted that God's commands were for his good, and so disobeyed. All of God's commands and instructions are, in fact, for our own good. Moreover, the new creation God is making of us ultimately will transcend the need for obedience and we will simply be holy and charitable because God's Spirit so indwells us that being holy and charitable becomes our nature – and our joy. But until that ultimate sanctification and divination occurs (II Peter 1.4), we follow God's laws out of obedience.

Application Question #2. What specific areas of your life can you think of right now for which God's plan may differ from your own?

_____

_____

_____

_____

As we consider the specifics of God's plan for our life – beginning in Part III with taking a daily prayer time – obedience definitely exacts a price. Our obedience and willingness to lay aside our plans (recognize God's ownership of us) are the key to embracing God's plan. We are only going to be as good a disciple as we are willing to take these words to heart.

Fully Committed

How easy it is to think of ourselves as being a Christian in the sense of simply trying to be a nice person. Is to

---

Make-Believe Lord?

Sociologists of religion find a fascinating disconnect: while a vast majority of Americans self-identify themselves as "Christians," a majority of Americans act contrary to the moral teaching of the Bible, which of course contains God's instructions. No news in that the Church is full of sinners! But in some ways, Christianity has come to resemble a folk religion with little more practical import for our day to day lives than, say, believing in Santa Claus.

make Jesus lord of our life simply to decide to "be a nice guy"? In the first century being a Christian often had grave and immediate consequences. Many of Jesus' first disciples were eventually disowned by their families, kicked out of the synagogue, and often worse. Americans who frequently move see their parents little and often have few meaningful long-term friendships – and besides, have many, many ways to divert themselves – and can't really appreciate how losing family, friends and the synagogue was quite literally the end of their social world. A Jew becoming a disciple of Jesus in 1st century Palestine was like a Muslim becoming a disciple of Jesus in 21st century Iran: taking Jesus as your lord was usually tantamount to a social and familial death, if not a physical one. Making Jesus lord often came with a stiff price. Making Jesus lord also clearly implied becoming obedient to Jesus' teaching and commandments as well as actively seeking his will for one's life.

Of course, the reason people made Jesus their lord was because they first came to know him – even after his resurrection and ascension into heaven. Unquestionably, Christians generally had a deep experience of God and, in fact, much of the New Testament is incomprehensible without reference to this deep delight in being in God's presence. They also realized how following Jesus' commands, principally avoiding sin, becoming like Jesus and living for others, actually produced joy as well, even if such a path involved brutal persecution and death.

Do we want to limp along as *occasional* disciples, especially since having only one foot in means having one foot out of the door? Sooner or later, we must give our lives fully and irrevocably to him: we will save ourselves an immense amount of difficulty and suffering by making this choice today and re-affirming this choice everyday. Like St. Peter, taking Jesus as our lord won't insulate you from sin and failure, but it will allow God to do what he must in order to prepare us for an eternity of joy with him and his people.

Exercise. Take some time to reflect on whether you have made Jesus lord of your life. If you never have, there is no better time than right now. For myself, I find that I need to consciously re-assert Jesus' lordship over my life every day. Simply pray,

> Oh God, I give my life fully to you without reservation: I am yours. Be lord of my life.
> Take me, hold me, do with me as you see fit.
> In the name of the Father and of the Son and of the Holy Spirit, Amen.

Lesson 6 – Making Jesus Lord of Our Men's Group

He disciplines us for our good that we may share in his holiness.

Hebrews 12.10

This lesson may be omitted for any readers proceeding through this book on their own.

If we wish Jesus to use our men's group to disciple us, then, quite simply, we need to make Jesus lord of our men's group! This lesson first considers why men usually get involved in a men's group and then how to make Jesus lord of our men's group. In particular, we let Jesus take our men's group through a **Discipleship Phase** by making *Conversion*, *Transformation* and then *Mission* the group's **agenda** for the next year or so.

Why do you Belong?

Check the boxes next to the reasons for your participation in the group:

Friendship

    I was talked into it by some persuasive acquaintance

    Friendship with one or more members of the group

    The other guys are funny, engaging or entertaining

    I share strong common interests in sports, work, etc.

Spiritual Growth, Prayer & Service

    As a response to a deeper conversion I experienced or from some prompting by God

    Praying together

    Desire for spiritual growth and sustenance

    To gain a deeper understanding of Scripture and the Catholic faith

    Help and encouragement in mastering sin and being faithful to my family and work

    As a group with whom to serve others

Brotherhood in Christ

    Enjoyment of brotherly relationships not so much out of inter-personal affinity or common interests but explicitly out of our mutual love of Christ and as brothers in Christ

    Out of a desire to help, pray for, rejoice with, encourage, and love one another

Fellowship or *Buddy-ship*?

Most small groups develop some pattern of praying together, studying or discussing

> **Buddyship Blastoffs**
>
> ➤ Who is going to win the election?
> ➤ My golf game has really tanked . . .
> ➤ Gosh . . . our team should rule the playoffs!

some aspect of Scripture, Church Teaching or the spiritual life, and *fellowshipping*, i.e., simply enjoying one another. Discussing politics, sports, a common hobby, finances, our kids, or whatever can easily dominate the group's agenda. While friendship may draw us to a men's group, if that's the only thing keeping us there, "buddy-ship" may well dominate your group. Mark where on the line you think your group falls on the fellowship - buddyship scale:

Fellowship ←——————————————————————→ Buddyship

Does your group have room to improve in this area? How?

_____

_____

_____

Specifics of Making Jesus Lord of Our Men's Group

In addition to fellowship, men's groups under the lordship of Christ focus on:

1) *Conversion*
2) Prayer and Scripture study
3) Spiritual Growth (*Transformation*)
4) Fellowship
5) Encouragement and help in living God's plan for our life
6) Service (*Mission*)

These purposes further God's plan for our life as follows:

God's Plan for Our Life

Purposes of a Men's Group	Being With God & His People	Becoming Like Jesus	Loving Who God Loves
1. *Conversion*	√		
2. Prayer and Scripture Study	√	√	√
3. Spiritual Growth (*Transformation*)		√	
4. Fellowship	√		√
5. Encouragement and help in living God's Plan for our Life	√	√	√
6. Serving Others (*Mission*)			√

By making Jesus lord both of our lives and of our men's groups we maintain a focus on conversion. Prayer, transformation and mission are considered in Part II while the next couple of lessons are devoted to fellowship and encouraging one another.

Life Cycle of a Men's Group pursuing Discipleship

Most successful men's groups have three phases: Launch; Discipleship & Kingdom Living.

Phase I: Launch

Any group of men first has to become a group of men! Phase I of a men's group often involves men coming together as a way to respond more deeply to God or out of friendship for others in the group. Sometimes such groups begin on some kind of retreat or immediately following a men's conference. Groups are often short-lived that fail to seriously grapple with conversion issues and to allow God to deepen the friendships into brotherly relationships. Conversion establishes our life with God and his people. We enjoy God through sacramental worship, personal prayer and Scripture study. We enjoy one another through gathering together to worship at Mass and through personal relationships with others centered on Christ – like in our men's group! The sacraments, prayer, scripture study and fellowship are the wellsprings of Christian life. A successful group launch will lay, or strengthen, these foundations.

Phase II: Discipleship

Being changed into his likeness from one degree of glory to another   II Corinthians 3.18

Those groups that allow God to move them from a conversion of hearts to a transformation of lives and to ripen friendship into fellowship may be called *Discipleship Groups* or groups in a *Discipleship Phase*. Initial conversion yields an ongoing life with God enjoyed in the sacraments and through daily prayer and scripture reading. By explicitly forming and embracing a plan for discipleship, such groups greatly hasten God's action of transforming their lives. Teaching on brotherly relationships is often necessary to catalyze the rich fraternal life God desires for us. Finally, men in a Phase II group begin to love God's work and seriously examine God's call to join this work in some way, to the extent time permits beyond caring for their families.

While it is true that God's work of transforming us into the likeness of Jesus usually takes a lifetime, we normally experience tremendous growth during the Discipleship Phase. We really do begin to look like *new creations* (II Corinthians 5.15-17). We find new energy and joy in living the Christian life. People around us can tell something has changed for the good, although some may frown because we no longer enjoy dirty jokes, negative speech, etc.

Phase III: Kingdom Living

You, too, go into the vineyard   Matthew 20.4

The *Discipleship Phase* indeed brings out the new kind of life that God intends for us. Although at times we may face heavy adversity in terms of job loss, sickness, death, etc., our lives should be characterized by an inner joy. More and more, we should resemble sons of the Father. More and more, we should tap into God's power through prayer, sacraments and scripture study. More and more, we should experience a godly joy as we love others by God's power: God pours his love into our hearts through the Holy Spirit (Romans 5.5).

A successful discipleship phase doesn't necessarily produce saints immediately, but we will be much transformed and our relationships with each other should become much richer. These more mature groups are firmly centered on a life of prayer and brotherly relationships in which life with God and his people finds tangible expression. These mature fraternal groups also sometimes work together in serving others by sharing about Jesus with common friends, through a work of mercy such as volunteering at a soup kitchen, or by supporting the life of the parish, perhaps by being ushers together. The following chart summarizes these three phases.

	Main Purposes	Characteristics
Phase I Launch	• Conversion • Friendship	• *duration: usually 1-3 months* • *undertake some type of conversion-oriented study*
Phase II Discipleship	• Prayer & Scripture Study • Fellowship • Transformation	• *duration: 9-18 months* • *enjoy life with God thru prayer and with his people through fellowship* • *follow topical discipleship plan for implementing God's plan in our life*
Phase III Kingdom Living	• Prayer & Scripture Study • Fellowship • Ongoing help in living God's plan • Embracing Mission	• *duration: indefinite long-term (annual commitments)* • *enjoy life with God thru prayer and with his people through fellowship* • *continue to help each other live the fullness of God's plan thru discussing different aspects of our lives* • *provides a basic context for living God's plan* • *serve together*

Spiritual Goal Setting

Men like clear-cut goals and objectives. Identify and set spiritual goals. For example, one may aim at ½ hour per day of personal prayer and scripture study. However, we have to be careful to avoid a "performance mentality" of just *getting it done*. With daily prayer how easily can we just "cross it off our list" as another task done, rather than enjoying the presence of the living God! At the end of the day, Christianity is about *being*, not *doing*. When everything is said and done – *and there is much to say and do this side of heaven* - we will not be running around trying to hit performance targets, rather we will dwell in the presence of irresistible holiness, rapt in a perfect unending joy. Never forget that the ultimate target is a person or, rather, being with a Person.

The group's facilitator keeps the group focused on its primary objectives. This is true both in avoiding the "buddy-ship" syndrome but also in pressing on in embracing God's plan for our life. Like anything else requiring ongoing focus and effort, spiritual goal setting can quickly melt away into just another good intention. Group members should use the *Action Items* box at the end of each lesson to set goals for themselves and discuss their progress during the ensuing lesson.

Action Plan

Step 1 – Commit to It

Men's Group Discipleship Commitment

The highest priority in my life is being with God. I pledge to spend _____ minutes per day in prayer, scripture study or celebrating the Eucharist both to spend time with God but also to allow him to transform me into his image.

I want God to transform my life to become like Jesus in terms of:

- seeing myself and the world as God sees them
- taking on his character and his holiness
- loving others as God loves them
- living and praying for others to embrace God's plan for their lives

As Jesus' disciple, I want to have my *pattern of life* support and express God's work of transforming me. In particular, I want my *life choices*, *daily routine* and *relationships* with all those around me to reinforce and express my efforts to imitate Christ. To the extent I have time and resources beyond caring for my family, I want to devote myself to interceding for others, sharing the good news of God's plan with all who don't know him, helping others, and serving the life of the parish.

I believe that God will use this group of disciples to help me embrace his plan for my life. I pledge:

- to pray together with these men;
- to maintain confidentiality in order for us to freely discuss our spiritual struggles;
- to encourage them to live for God;
- to intercede regularly for each member of this group; and
- to love them as brothers.

I plan on meeting with the group for the next _____ months, approximately ____ times per month. I realize that unforeseen circumstances may prevent me from meeting every time the group meets, but I plan to make my attendance in the group a very high priority.

By: _____   Date: _____

In our world super-charged with the promise of many pleasures, filled with demanding jobs, and overflowing with all kinds of other stresses and challenges, discipleship doesn't happen automatically: we must decide for it. Many groups make a group commitment; discuss the above commitment before each member signs and dates it.

Step 2 – Tune-up

How does your group fare in terms of some basic group dynamics? Evaluate your group's dynamics by filling out the following table:

Area	Group Discipleship Dynamic	Rate Your Group
Basics Skills	Attendance, prep and enthusiasm	
	Maintain group focus	
	Balanced participation by all group members	
Team Captain	Servant Leadership	
	Facilitator Duties	
Game Plan	Focus on personal application, not theological enquiry	
	Pose universal questions; Seek individual answers	
	Recognize that "one size doesn't fit all" in terms of personal prayer time, use of our time, individual gifting, etc.	
Teamwork	Zeal for pursuing God's plan for our lives	
	Strive together as peers	
	Love and pray for one another	
Making Plays	Make group a "safe place" to share about our goals, challenges, failures, and successes	
	Role of goal setting and accountability	
	Safeguard of personal autonomy in decision making	
	Tackling deep-seated problems & finishing strong	

Discuss how each member rates the group. Does your group have a facilitator? Does everyone clearly understand the facilitator's role? Should your group review some of the discipleship dynamics?

_____

_____

_____

_____

Your group may wish to consult the Appendix on Discipleship Dynamics, which is organized according to the above table, at your next meeting.

Step 3 - Basic Construction: Allowing God to use our Men's Group to Disciple Us

Certain items are necessary to call a structure a house. Walls, a roof, a bathroom, a kitchen, eating area and bedroom characterize the smallest bungalows and the greatest mansions. Similarly, any disciple possesses certain basic elements. You are now ready to move into Part II of this book, which considers concrete discipleship lessons – applicable to every disciple - centering around:

> ➢ Basic Training (prayer)
> ➢ Equipping for Battle (overcoming challenges)
> ➢ Transformation (becoming like Jesus)
> ➢ Embracing Mission (loving whom God loves)

Part II   Being a Disciple: Embracing God's Plan for Our Lives

Lesson 1 - Foundations

Every one then who hears these words of mine and does them will be like a wise man who built his house upon the rock; and the rain fell, and the floods came, and the winds blew and beat upon that house, but it did not fall, because it had been founded on the rock.   Matthew 7.24-25

The foundation for being a disciple is, first of all, conversion to God – in fact, *daily* conversion, inasmuch as conversion entails repenting of our *daily* sins, asking for God's forgiveness and making Jesus lord of our life. We are drawn to a loving God who promises us the indescribable joy of living with him and his people. We delight in the basic truths of our faith: God's tremendous fatherly love, Jesus' saving sacrifice, and the power of the Holy Spirit. The grace of the Eucharist and Confession renew and sustain our conversion. Conversion implies a life of prayer and transformation into the image of God's only son and issues forth in doing the works, or embracing the mission, of Jesus – all of which yield great happiness. Prayer is void without conversion, transformation dead absent prayer, and mission possible only with all three. Finally, being a disciple requires a wholehearted focus, requiring that we simplify our lives.

The Prodigal Son, Rembrandt

Daily Conversion

If you confess with your lips that Jesus is Lord and believe in your heart that God raised him from the dead, you will be saved   Romans 10.19

In professing faith at baptism and confirmation, we "confess" our faith and are "saved" from our sins by accepting Christ's work of salvation. We can profess this faith only after rejecting evil and the works of the Evil One ("repenting"). We make Jesus lord by giving our lives and obedience fully to him. Conversion immediately makes possible life with God and his people. Since all of us continue to sin, fail in obedience and take back our lives from God, ongoing, even daily, conversion is necessary. In fact, we Catholics devote a whole season of the year – Lent - to conversion!

Discussion Question. Many Catholic men have particular difficulty making Jesus lord of our life. We really like doing our own thing, calling the shots, as it were. You may wish to review Part I, Lesson 5. What areas of your life do you have difficulty submitting to Christ? In what areas do you struggle to be obedient?

_____

_____

_____

_____

Entering into the Very Life of God

Grace is a *participation in the life of God*. It introduces us into the intimacy of Trinitarian life: by Baptism the Christian participates in the grace of Christ, the Head of his Body. As an "adopted son" he can henceforth call God "Father," in union with the only Son. He receives the life of the Spirit who breathes charity into him and who forms the Church.   Spiritual progress tends toward ever more intimate union with Christ.   CCC 1997, 2014

Holiness

> *Strive . . . for the holiness without which no one will see God.*   Hebrews 12.14

In addition to being profoundly loving, God is holy – and holiness is absolutely required to come into God's presence. We must be properly dressed, so to speak. We have to be clothed in the holiness of God, to have the smelly repugnance of our sinfulness washed away[3]. The price of such a cleaning? Just ask for forgiveness – but you have to ask. The way to keep clean? Ask for help – in fact, become a habitual asker for help. Seek God's grace through the sacraments and by asking him to give more of the Holy Spirit. This incessant posture of pleading for God's help is the sense of the "pray constantly" in the I Thessalonians 5.17 passage.

Read Exodus 33.18-23. Was Moses fit to see God? Why or why not?

_____

_____

_____

Sinning and failing to ask God's forgiveness blocks and undermines our personal prayer. That's one of the reasons why spiritual writers through the ages recommend a daily examination of conscience, i.e., scrutinizing yourself for ways in which you may have offended God or others or have failed to love and serve others, which we will consider later.

Confession & Eucharist

Disciples are devoted to spending time with God and his people. God makes fully present the grace of his saving sacrifice through the Mass, which is the "source and summit of our faith." In the Mass we also experience and express the deeply communal life to which God calls us. For our own good, God requires us to worship together at Mass every Sunday, a day made holy and which makes us holy by the Resurrection.

Confession is the sacrament of conversion, through which we are prepared for our first Holy Communion and which strengthens and restores our communion with God and his people. Since we sin against God, which includes his body the Church, God fully restores us through the sacrament of Confession.

We live in a world that glorifies all kinds of sin. Notice how just about any newspaper trumpets lust, greed, envy, pride, etc. We are easily seduced. When we sin, we repent and go to confession. Do you have any sins to repent of? Do you need to get to confession? The Church requires us to confess once per year and whenever we commit mortal sin; discipleship requires frequent confession, particularly as we struggle to root out sin and to grow in charity.

> **Worship with Reverence and Awe**
>
> [18]For you have not come to what may be touched, a blazing fire, and darkness, and gloom, and a tempest, [19] and the sound of a trumpet, and a voice whose words made the hearers entreat that no further messages be spoken to them. [20] For they could not endure the order that was given, "If even a beast touches the mountain, it shall be stoned." [21] Indeed, so terrifying was the sight that Moses said, "I tremble with fear."
>
> [22] But you have come to Mount Zion and to the city of the living God, the heavenly Jerusalem, and to innumerable angels in festal gathering, [23] and to the assembly of the first-born who are enrolled in heaven, and to a judge who is God of all, and to the spirits of just men made perfect, [24] and to Jesus, the mediator of a new covenant, and to the sprinkled blood that speaks more graciously than the blood of Abel.
>
> [28] . . . Let us offer to God acceptable worship, with reverence and awe; [29] for our God is a consuming fire.   Hebrews 12

Simplicity of Life: Eliminating Competition

You are worried and distracted by many things; there is need of only one thing.   Lk 10.41

Crowding one's life with too many pursuits, pursuing a worthy goal too intensely, and cluttering up with mostly harmless past-times are among the greatest blocks to following Jesus. The antidote that saints have prescribed through the ages is to *simplify your life*.

Pruning Pursuits. Our society fosters an incredibly prosperous life, but also the hyper-growth of weeds both in the heart and the garden of free time. For many, the values of the work-place also nurture un-healthy growth in our hearts. Some of the "weeds" are normally attractive plants that rise to grotesque heights. Such plants come to overshadow and choke, rather than complement, our life with God and his people. Working too many hours is an example of a normally healthy part of our lives growing out of control and choking out our prayer lives or time with family. Perhaps we want a bigger house or a more prestigious job. Over time, we come to adjust our mind and values to what we actually do. One's job soon forms one's basic identity rather than being how we support our family and exercise God-given talents. In practice, being overly concerned about our studies or our job (or pursuit of pleasure, desire for belongings, quest for raising perfect kids, bitterness over some problem, etc.) prevents us from being a wholehearted disciple.

Eliminating Clutter. Cluttering our days is a form of self-indulgence that defuses our focus, often weakens our personality and turns us inward, and always wastes time. How do you clutter your day? Check the boxes that apply:

- ☐ Video gaming including computer & phone puzzles
- ☐ Reading newspapers and magazines
- ☐ Emailing, texting, instant messaging (excessive)
- ☐ Checking weather, sports scores, stocks, etc.
- ☐ Web-surfing; ebaying
- ☐ Watching sports highlights and news
- ☐ Using Myspace, Facebook, YouTube
- ☐ Taking long showers, daydreaming
- ☐ Other: _____
- ☐ Other: _____

While there is often a recreational and sometimes even a social benefit to these activities, they come the clutter up our days, creating needless activity that distracts us from our general overall focus of living for God and others. Bottom Line:

If we haven't simplified our life enough to have a daily prayer time and attend Mass every Sunday, Jesus isn't Lord of our life and we are hardly his disciple.

Discussion Question. Which of your pursuits need pruning in order to pray daily even just for 15 minutes and get to Mass on Sunday?

_____

_____

Basis for Prayer, Transformation and Mission

Conversion, maintaining holiness and keeping our lives simple and focused on being disciples is the basis for the overall objectives of discipleship, which are covered in the rest of this book. The next lesson addresses a major obstacle to maintaining holiness for most Christian men: lust, particularly in the form of soft and hard pornography. Then the next section, *Basic Training*, helps us establish a life of prayer, without which we cannot be disciples of Christ. *Equipping for Battle* discusses the major challenges to being disciples and how to overcome them, which is followed by sections introducing *Transformation* and *Our Mission*.

Action Items

- ☐ Prayer/scripture reading of _____ minutes per day
- ☐ Pray for group member: _____ regarding: _____
- ☐ Eliminate clutter by _____

Lesson 2 - Purity of Heart

Blessed are the pure in heart, for they shall see God.   Matthew 5.8

This lesson will consider, briefly, an aspect of holiness, one of the foundations we considered in the last lesson, because of its importance in developing a prayer life, which we will take up in the next section. Scripture teaches us that even on this side of heaven, God, the Holy Spirit, dwells within our hearts, which is made possible by the holiness we receive through Jesus' redeeming and sanctifying death on the cross (See John 14-15, Romans 8, and I Corinthians 3 and 6, among other biblical texts). As we noted in the last lesson, holiness is a requirement for being in God's presence, whether in receiving the Eucharist, being filled with his Holy Spirit, or, finally, in heaven. Purity of heart speaks to the holiness of our sexuality[4]. Sexual immorality stands opposite from purity of heart, destroys our holiness, and renders us incapable of being filled with God's Spirit, let alone seeing God.

Lust drives most sexual immorality. Among the sins of men in this age, lust may not be the worse – pride remains the perennial champ – yet lust may do the most wide-spread damage and be the most pervasive. Following the sexual revolution of the 60s and its mainstreaming in the 70s and 80s, the last two decades have seen a more mature flowering of a *culture of lust* as soft-porn has become embedded throughout television, movies, magazines, and advertising. The plots of many television shows and movies also seem to turn on sexual immorality and even on what used to be considered sexual deviancy. Today's hard-porn has grown in intensity as much as it has in immediacy of access, the latter primarily through the internet but also through so-called "adult TV". Perhaps pornography is the predominate form of lust today, at least among men. According to various studies and surveys, the majority of Christian men succumb to this most easily hidden vice.

Only a Few "Kid-Clicks" Away

How easy is it to find internet porn? True Story: a six year old boy was wondering what the word "humping" means, a word his older brothers had bandied about. Googling a few six-year-old misspellings of this word – when no one was looking - brought up extremely graphic depictions of, well, humping!

Make no mistake. If we wish to experience the Lord in prayer, grow spiritually, and gain that glorious and indescribable joy of heaven– and avoid the opposite result of spiritual death and eternal separation from God – we must give no quarter to any sin. Lust is singled out here inasmuch as most men struggle with it. In the words of Paul, "those who belong to Christ have crucified the flesh with its passions and desires" (Galatians 5.24, cf. 2.24).

Lust is disordered desire for, or inordinate enjoyment of, sexual pleasure. Sexual pleasure is morally disordered when sought for itself, isolated from its procreative and unitive purposes.
Catechism of the Catholic Church, 2351

The Purpose of Purity

Do you not know that your body is a temple of the Holy Spirit within you,
which you have from God?

I Corinthians 6.19

Baptism changes our fundamental identity: we literally become members of Christ's body and temples of his Holy Spirit. God dearly wants an almost incomprehensible intimacy with us. The indwelling of his Spirit is a *personal* intimacy; spiritual growth in one sense amounts to awakening to this living and personal relationship with God. Read the passage in I Corinthians 6:11,13-20.

1. This passage speaks of an amazing unity that baptism brings us into with God. What does this passage say about illicit sexual intercourse?

   _____

   _____

   _____

2. How does illicit sexual intercourse undermine our relationship with God and his ability to dwell in us?

   _____

   _____

   _____

The Problem of Porn

Every one who looks at a woman lustfully has already committed adultery with her in his heart.

Matthew 5.28

Why is porn – or any form of lust – bad? What we will say in this section applies to lust in general and virtually all types of sexual immorality. We have already noted that sexual immorality undermines our deepest purposes – being filled with the Holy Spirit and being with God in heaven. Lust and sexual immorality cause harm by:

1. destroying our relationship with God (as with any serious sin);
2. competing with – and undermining – our appetite for being with God;
3. making us view our spouses (or girlfriends), and women in general, as objects of sexual gratification, which undermines our ability for intimate and unitive sexual intercourse, and undermines our enjoyment of sexual intercourse with our wives inasmuch as viewing porn makes us long for "perfect bodies";
4. undermining our wives (or girlfriends) trust in us;
5. addicting us in the same way one becomes addicted to alcohol or drug abuse; and

6. making us deeply narcissistic.

Lusting amounts to viewing women as objects of sexual gratification in a way that usually overwhelms seeing their potential as daughters of God, temples of the Holy Spirit, and sisters in Christ. How sweet is true friendship with other men and women based on our

joint identity in Christ and the infusion of the Holy Spirit; how wretched the power of lust to undermine our capacity for such friendship! Rather than the sexual fulfillment glorified in our culture, lust isolates us from those in whom we are made to delight (God and our spouse) and turns us deeply inward, rendering us less able to enjoy true friendship with others. Moreover, lust's addictive character coupled with free and instant online access to pornography, or simply masturbating, make it particularly difficult to overcome. Jesus' teaching cuts directly to the deadly crux of the matter. Read Matthew 5.27-30.

1. What occasions do you think 1st century Palestinians had to "look at a woman lustfully"?

_____

_____

_____

2. What imagery does Jesus use to express how to deal with lust? How does the harshness of this imagery convey to us how deadly lust can be?

_____

_____

_____

The Battle for Purity

If your right eye causes you to sin, pluck it out and throw it away.   Matthew 5.29

The Catholic Church forbids self-mutilation in dealing with sin. However, Jesus enjoins us to battle ferociously against the sin of lust. The best way to kill lawn weeds is to grow healthy grass which chokes them to death. Developing a prayer and sacramental life (see section on Basic Training) and robust Christian friendships (such as the ones in a men's group), cultivating the fruit of the Spirit and allowing God to transform us into the image of his son (see section on Transformation), and filling our lives up with his mission (see section on Our Mission) will, essentially, fill our hearts with the deeply satisfying things of God. This "Focus on the Things of God" strategy is helpful in combating all kinds of ingrained patterns of sin.

We also need very practical tactics in overcoming temptations, especially in combating lust in the midst of our culture of lust. The most common areas of struggle include:
1. Lust of the Eyes (lustfully appraising women around us);
2. Pornography & Sexual Fantasies;
3. Masturbation; and
4. Extra-marital sexual relations.

Our foundation is battling any area of sin is asking for God's help and his forgiveness, particularly through the sacrament of confession. Grieve over your sins (but not despairing, for we must trust in God's grace even in the face of great challenges; see also Lesson 13 and the Appendix on Discipleship Dynamics). Seek out Mary's intercession; she is the patroness of purity. Making ourselves accountable to a men's group – that is, pledging to confess any sins to the men in the group on a confidential basis – or to a close male friend are very powerful tactics. Porn filters as well as accountability software are excellent on-line tools. For a comprehensive list of resources, see http://www.dads.org/strugglewithporn.asp.

Discussion Questions

1. Read Luke 1.26-38. In what ways is Mary a model "temple of the Holy Spirit"? What level of purity and holiness must she have possessed?

   _____

   _____

   _____

2. Sometimes thinking of your mother watching you can be a helpful deterrent to lustful sins. Would you find it more helpful to think of your biological mother in this regard, or of Mary, your mother by virtue of becoming a brother of Jesus through baptism? Why?

   _____

   _____

   _____

   _____

Action Items

- ☐ Prayer/scripture reading of _____ minutes per day
- ☐ Pray for group member: _____ regarding: _____
- ☐ Take these steps to battle lust _____ ;
  _____ ; & _____

Basic Training
(Prayer)

Landauer Altar, Albrecht Dürer

How lovely is your dwelling place, O LORD of hosts!
My soul longs, indeed it faints for the courts of the LORD;
my heart and my flesh sing for joy to the living God

Psalm 84:1-2

Lesson 3 – Prayer: Beholding God's Face

One thing have I asked of the LORD, that will I seek after; that I may dwell in the house of the LORD all the days of my life, to behold the beauty of the LORD.

Psalm 27.4

Often, only need or anxiety drives many of us to pray, or, more aptly, to cry out, "Oh God – Help!" It's easy for men to think of a life of prayer as a "women's thing." Doesn't prayer connote weakness? After all, we like to do it ourselves and figure things out on our own. Sure, God has a role, but we don't want to trouble him unless we get into real trouble.

Such a mindset may capture how our culture views us, but as Christian men we should know better. Only saints are in heaven, and if we wish to get there we need God's help in small things and great – indeed, all things that make for holiness and charity. For our sanctity only comes from God. Moreover, as much as we might enjoy sports and good food, our deepest appetites are for God himself – simply being with and enjoying the King of Kings, the Lord of Lords, the One enthroned on Cherubim, the Captain of the Armies of Israel, but also the Author of Beauty, the One of dazzling brilliance and glory, the One before whom every knee shall bend and every tongue confess that Jesus Christ is Lord. The richness of God's presence is so incomparably great that Scriptural visions can only resort to descriptions such as magnificent feasting, lavish riches, flowing water and dazzling light.

Remember, King David was no sissy, but rather the most terrible and feared of warriors and a brilliant general. And yet he literally danced in ecstasy before the ark of God as it was being brought up to Jerusalem (II Samuel 6.1-5) and wrote or inspired many of the sublime psalms that are quoted throughout this study. David was a man's man who rejoiced in God's presence. Not only that, but King David attributed his strength and power to God: King David relied on God for his power – a power that came from being in God's presence.

Prayer, in fact, has three principal components related to being in God's presence[5]. **Contemplation** involves knowing our Father's love as well as gazing upon his beauty and glory. In beholding his face, we see the personification of love, mercy, justice, goodness and God's other attributes. **Thanksgiving** is the natural response to beholding God's goodness to us. **Intercession** is also our natural response to perceiving God's will, which can be best understood by spending time with God in prayer and reading Scripture. Of course, you don't have to be in God's presence to thank him or intercede – but it helps!

The Ultimate Prayer Life

The ultimate life of prayer is our promised eternal life in heaven, when we will stand before God. Church tradition refers to this as the beatific vision:

This mystery of blessed communion with God and all who are in Christ is beyond all understanding and description. Scripture speaks of it in images: life, light, peace, wedding feast, wine of the kingdom, the Father's house, the heavenly Jerusalem, paradise: "no eye has seen, nor ear heard, nor the heart of man conceived, what God has prepared for those who love him." CCC 1027-9

It's easy to think that contemplative prayer outside of heaven is limited to monks and nuns who devote their entire lives to prayer, locked away in monasteries. And yet the Church teaches that all Catholics should taste at least some of the sweetness of God's love and beauty (Ps. 27.4; 34.8), despite the rough and tumble of studying, raising children, being married, working, and generally living in a busy world filled with many pressing demands and absorbing distractions. Indeed, John Paul II requires that parishes become schools of prayer, where "the meeting with Christ is expressed not just in imploring help but also in thanksgiving, praise, adoration, contemplation, listening and ardent devotion, until the heart truly 'falls in love'"[6].

If contemplative prayer is a foretaste of being with God in heaven, then it is a foretaste of experiencing his love, tenderness, and committed-ness to us as beloved sons of the Father and brothers of the Son. Prayer can equally be a foretaste of the wonders and incredible joy of beholding God's splendor. Fully entrusting ourselves to God and placing our lives in his hand opens up our hearts to the warmth of his love. As our emotional temperaments vary, our affective experience of God's love varies. For one it may be the feeling of absolute serenity, for another the sweetness of being forgiven. For some, a certain unfathomable inward joy, for others a quiet serenity or confidence. Some will experience the "jubilation" of King David dancing before God, others the quiet glow of adoration. One person's experience of God's love may vary from day to day and from season to season. Some may be so damaged by personal sin that it takes many years to learn to trust God and begin experiencing the richness of his love.

First Steps

Success in developing and experiencing some level of contemplative prayer depends on the following factors (among others):

1 – having a vision and an understanding of contemplative prayer
2 – developing a hunger for being with God
3 – adopting and maintaining a habit of daily prayer
4 – maintaining a minimal level of sanctity by repenting of any and all sin on a daily basis and accessing redemptive and regenerative grace through attending Mass and Confession.

The purpose of the next two lessons is to help you develop a rudimentary or very basic level of contemplative prayer, particularly as it relates to beholding God's splendor. I believe that most people should find with some regularity a sweetness and delight in God's presence by praying contemplatively on a daily basis, even if such prayer is as brief as fifteen minutes and involves only the simple steps discussed in this and the following lessons[7]. Of course, there is much, much more that God has for some of us in this life and all of us in heaven. It is worth noting that sustaining a lifetime habit of even fifteen or twenty minutes of daily prayer depends upon putting God first in our life and giving him free complete authority to make us holy and loving like himself, in very practical and tangible ways, some of which are discussed in the next two sections of this book on "Equipping for Battle" and "Transformation."

Embracing even a simple prayer life supported by a lifetime of discipleship yields joy in prayer and a slow but steady transformation into the very likeness of God. As C.S. Lewis notes, God is making us beings of dazzling brilliance, filled with a holiness and love resembling his own. Indeed, we are becoming "partakers of the divine nature" (II Peter 1.4). To be sure, for most of us this transformation will take a lifetime and our "unutterable and indescribable joy" will be complete only in heaven. And yet here and now God lavishes on us foretastes of heaven, and our access to him and his transforming power is limited only by our desire.

Joy Beyond All Understanding

By his death and Resurrection, Jesus Christ has "opened" heaven to us. The life of the blessed consists in the full and perfect possession of the fruits of the redemption accomplished by Christ. He makes partners in his heavenly glorification those who have believed in him and remained faithful to his will. Heaven is the blessed community of all who are perfectly incorporated into Christ.

This mystery of blessed communion with God and all who are in Christ is beyond all understanding and description. Scripture speaks of it in images: life, light, peace, wedding feast, wine of the kingdom, the Father's house, the heavenly Jerusalem, paradise: "no eye has seen, nor ear heard, nor the heart of man conceived, what God has prepared for those who love him."

Because of his transcendence, God cannot be seen as he is, unless he himself opens up his mystery to man's immediate contemplation and gives him the capacity for it. The Church calls this contemplation of God in his heavenly glory "the beatific vision":

> How great will your glory and happiness be, to be allowed to see God, to be honored with sharing the joy of salvation and eternal light with Christ your Lord and God, . . . to delight in the joy of immortality in the Kingdom of heaven with the righteous and God's friends.   CCC 1026-8

Living the Life of Prayer

1. Do you have any male role models for a strong prayer life? What impresses you about them? Do they seem to enjoy prayer and to find strength from God?

   _____

   _____

   _____

2. What did God making King David so mighty in battle have to do with God's plan for Israel? What types of power does God give us?

_____

_____

_____

3. What's the biggest thing holding you back from praying on a daily basis? How can you overcome this obstacle?

_____

_____

_____

Action Items

☐ Prayer/scripture reading of _____ minutes per day
☐ Pray for group member: _____ regarding: _____
☐ Memorize Psalm 27.4

Lesson 4 - Contemplating God: Beautiful Beyond Description

Rejoice always, pray constantly, give thanks in all circumstances; for this is the will of God in Christ Jesus for you.   I Thessalonians 5.16-18

God is said to be beautiful and glorious beyond description: out of Zion, the perfection of beauty, God shines forth (Ps 50.2). In addition to experiencing God's love, contemplation involves gazing

upon God's beauty and glory[8]. Contemplating, in the sense of recognizing and enjoying God's beauty and glory, may involve as little as five or ten minutes of prayer or "gazing." Of course, contemplation can also verge on the mystical, where one becomes completely absorbed in beholding God, even for long stretches of time. This lesson is concerned with everyday, shorter and less intense moments of enjoying God which are available to all Catholics during their times of personal prayer and in sacramental worship.

Let's begin by trying to get to the bottom of our own experiences of beauty, which may help us to contemplate God's beauty. So take some time to consider what you find beautiful – for at least five minutes in some quiet place, close your eyes and think about beauty, about persons, things, and experiences or whatever you associate with beauty. Jot down what comes to mind in a free-flowing manner.

_____

_____

_____

_____

_____

_____

_____

_____

_____

_____

_____

Describe your greatest encounters of beauty over the last several months[9]

1. _____

2. _____

3. _____

Beauty has a certain element of mystery to it – why are mountains beautiful? Describe why chocolate tastes good and I'll tell you why something's beautiful! Beauty is just beautiful, like chocolate is simply delicious. So, what is God's beauty like?

Suppose your greatest encounter with beauty is a sunset over the ocean. Way better than a mud puddle, right? Well, that sunset is like a mud puddle compared to God's beauty! Or to compare the beauty of a cooing baby with gazing on the Father is like comparing a candle to the sun.

The same type of analogy holds for God's other attributes, such as his love, goodness, mercy, power, knowledge, creativity, and justice. Can everyday

experiences tell us something about God's characteristics? Consider a mom rescuing her baby from a burning house as a very pale comparison to God's love for us and parents denying themselves luxuries and even necessities in order to save for their kids' college tuition as one for goodness. Magnifying such love a gazillion times gives us some idea of God's love for us and to what extremes he will go for our sake. Consider some everyday experiences that, by comparison, can help us understand some of God's attributes:

> Loving ____*taking out the garbage* _____

> Kind _____

> Good _____

> Merciful _____

> Powerful _____

> Knowing _____

> Creative _____

> Just _____

> Awesome _____

> Glorious _____

> Funny _____

> Humble _____

> Holy[10] _____

Well, God is the ultimate version, quite literally the personification, of each of these adjectives, all at once! We are all attracted to kind faces, just people, awesome sights. In heaven we will see kindness, justice, and awe itself, literally emanating from the face of God, together with all his other attributes. A good way to contemplate God is by considering his goodness, love, humility, etc. and then praising these divine attributes over and over again. I often begin worshiping God by simply saying over and over again, "God you are so _____," filling in the blank with one of God's attributes. I repeat the phrase slowly and meditatively (silently or out loud, whatever is more comfortable). Sometimes I imagine the saints and angels of God surrounding his

---

Worship in Spirit?

Jesus said to her, "Woman, believe me, the hour is coming when neither on this mountain nor in Jerusalem will you worship the Father. You worship what you do not know; we worship what we know, for salvation is from the Jews. But the hour is coming, and now is, when the true worshipers will worship the Father in spirit and truth, for such the Father seeks to worship him. God is spirit, and those who worship him must worship in spirit and truth."   John 4.21-24

---

throne together chanting the same phrase in worship, thousands upon thousands. As you grow in your life of prayer and ask God for more and more of his Holy Spirit, he will reveal to you more and more of his beauty and glory.

Living the Life of Prayer

1. Pick one of your encounters with beauty you listed earlier in this lesson. Describe what you found beautiful. What particularly appealed to you?

    _____

    _____

    _____

    _____

    _____

2. Which of God's attributes most attracts you? Why?

    _____

    _____

    _____

    _____

    _____

Action Items

☐ Prayer/scripture reading of _____ minutes per day

☐ Pray for group member: _____ regarding: _____

☐ Memorize I Thessalonians 5.16-18

Lesson 5 - Imagine Being in Heaven

To take a different perspective, picture being in heaven with God for a few minutes. After all, if prayer is being with God, in heaven is where we see him face to face. So thinking about heaven can help our prayer life on earth. How do you imagine heaven?

1. _____

2. _____

3. _____

Perhaps the most vivid account of eternal life with God in the Scriptures is found in Revelation 4.1-11. What's going on in heaven, according to this passage?

_____

_____

_____

_____

_____

What the saints and doctors of the church tell us is that, at least to a limited degree, God wants us to enjoy the same sweetness of gazing on his holiness and grandeur, the radiant beauty of all his attributes, that we see the saints and angels enjoying in heaven here in Revelation. I can't tell you mechanically how God brings us this wonder and sweetness. What I do know is that when we prayerfully think about God's goodness and beauty, somehow the Holy Spirit makes us see and even experience it! This is true whether we are praying privately in the morning, entering into worship at Mass, meditating upon the rich mercy of Christ in reciting the Rosary, singing worship songs, reading about God's holiness in Scripture, or looking at icons.

The last several chapters of Revelation further describe what heaven will be like. List five important things about heaven described in Revelation 19.1-9, 21.1-7 and in 21.22-22.5:

1. _____

2. _____

3. _____

4. _____

5. _____

In addition to basking in God's love, heaven will dazzle and mesmerize us with his glory and beauty – of which we shall never tire or have enough. In fact, the Lord wants us to experience this joy, *to some degree*, right now, in both our personal prayer life and our life of corporate worship centered on the Mass.

Can our contemplation of God *really* be like gazing on him in heaven? Yes and no. No, probably not on any kind of regular basis; even St. Paul only sporadically experienced being "caught up into heaven" in his prayer. After all, the Lord gives us each responsibilities and entrusts us with his mission while we live on earth (as we shall further investigate in the lessons ahead). Yet we can experience *imperfectly* at least some of the joy of being with God in heaven.

HUNGRY? At the end of the day, how richly and deeply we contemplate God is proportional to how badly we wish to be with him. The more deeply we wish to see God, the more God reveals himself. We have to translate our desires into the practical steps outlined in the next section. God is there for the asking but, again, we do have to ask.

As we spend more and more time with him, God transforms us into his own likeness, that of Jesus. Ultimately, he so changes us that an irrepressible love for others and hunger to draw them to God supplements, and even replaces, loving others out of obligation. An overwhelming desire to be with God replaces praying out of a sense of duty. Just as Jesus loves spending time with the Father, so will we.

Worship at a Rock Concert?

As a sixteen year old I idolized the musician Eric Clapton – together with tens of millions of adoring fans around the world. Together with 40,000 fans, I chanted his name - Clapton, Clapton, Clapton – longing, hungering for an encore. After soaking up this adulation many long minutes backstage, Clapton finally sprang through the haze of smoke and dazzling lights onto stage. The chanting erupted into shrieks and frenzied clapping until well into the encore song.

Compare adulation of rock stars with Revelation 4.

Helps in Contemplative Prayer

The practical exercises above considering God's beauty and other attributes and what heaven will be like are primers for contemplation; hopefully they help cultivate our sense of what is beautiful (and glorious). Let me summarize a few more practical pointers:

1. Take the time to seek God: **ask God to bring you closer and to help you simply to be with him, to experience his love, and behold his beauty and glory; ask God to pour out his Holy Spirit** – his very presence - on you. You can do this right now; you may also find some help from your parish's prayer group.
2. Meditate and **consider how much God loves us**. Consider how he draws us to himself as discussed in the first three lessons of this book. Read through the gospels and seek out books on God's love at your local Catholic bookstore.
3. We need to **let God change us** – it may take a while before we are pining and longing for God's presence all the time. Practice makes perfect. Consistency is important. Keep on praying and seeking God on a daily basis, even when we don't see direct fruit. Developing a solid prayer life takes time!
4. **Sing worshipful songs.** A fine singing voice isn't necessary to worship God in song. Find a few songs that you particularly like, get the music, and begin a personal prayer time by singing. Sing softly if you are embarrassed or to avoid distracting others. St. Augustine famously teaches: he who sings prays twice.
5. **Set aside some time for silence**, to simply be with God and listen to him. You may wish to find a beautiful spot or a quiet place.
6. **Pray through God's attributes**, as discussed above, taking just one or two at a time, considering the ways in which God so fully exemplifies the attribute, all the while praising God over and over again, slowly: "God, you are holy"; or "God your power is without measure"; etc.
7. Using an approach similar to praising God's attributes, **pray through the titles of God** as found in Scripture. Consult your local Catholic bookstore for one of the many books on this topic as well as on God's attributes[11].
8. **Pray through the Psalms.** Read through them and note ones that you particularly like. The Liturgy of the Hours, based on the Psalms, is also a brilliant method.

My own experience of contemplative prayer has been fed by two primary sources: reading and meditating on Scripture and receiving the outpouring of the Holy Spirit through the Charismatic Renewal. I usually sing worshipful songs to begin a time of contemplation. Though everyone may not feel drawn to charismatic prayer, the Holy Spirit is given to all of us in baptism and confirmation (e.g., John 1.32-33, Acts 1.4-5, 2.1-4, 10.43-48). The Holy Spirit dwells in us (e.g., John 14.17, Romans 8.1-17, and I Corinthians 6.19) and is our access to God's presence in prayer (e.g., John 4.23-24, II Corinthians 3.16-18). In other words, the Holy Spirit is the basis for contemplative prayer[12] and we should continually seek to be filled more and more regardless of our interest (or lack thereof) in charismatic gifts. Let's make our own John Paul II's daily prayer: *Come Holy Spirit.*

I believe that asking for and receiving a greater outpouring of God's Spirit provides us something of an initial shortcut to the deeper experience of God in prayer that is described as contemplation. Yet, even if God plunks you down in the middle of the heavenly feast, how easily does everyday life and our own sinfulness interrupt such delight. The foundational work described by the great mystics such as John of the Cross and Teresa of Avila has to be done some how or other, sooner or later, in order to establish a robust contemplative life. See the For Further Study section. The upcoming section on "Transformation," Lessons 18-25, summarizes God's foundational work of transforming our lives to become like Christ's, which, in turn, deepens and perfects our appetite and ability to contemplate (and be with) God.

Living the Life of Prayer

1. What do you most look forward to about heaven? Why?

_____

_____

_____

_____

_____

2. Why is God's willingness to reveal himself to us in prayer in part dependent upon how badly we desire to be in his presence, on his terms?

_____

_____

_____

_____

Action Items

- ☐ Prayer/scripture reading of _____ minutes per day
- ☐ Pray for group member: _____ regarding: _____
- ☐ Read through Psalms 4, 17, 19, 26-27, 42-43, 73, 84, and 104

Lesson 6 - Thanksgiving Prayer

Vatican Altar Piece, Raphael

Thanksgiving prayer, like contemplative prayer, most naturally flows from being in the presence of God. Rather than appreciating his beauty and glory, thanksgiving is the response of acknowledging God's goodness. The basic human reflex of thanksgiving is what happens if a truck stops at your house and somebody unloads twenty bags of gold at your door: who do I thank? As we stand in God's presence, we recognize his many fabulous gifts to us and – at least on a good day[13] – overflow with thanksgiving.

What to give thanks for? The answer to this question is in many ways the key to life. If we don't have a foundational awe and appreciation of God's creation – beginning actually with ourselves, whatever our circumstances or limitations – we're probably not going to get very far in our relationship with God. God made us conscious – aware of ourselves and, more importantly, of God. He made us capable of appreciating goodness, truth and beauty. Finally, as discussed in Lesson 3, God invites us into an eternity of joy with him – for which he personally pays the price and into which he personally guides us. Oh, and did I mention giving us the Holy Spirit?

We may enjoy rather pleasant earthly circumstances or be a quadriplegic (or caring for one). We may have appeared on the Oprah Winfrey show as the Victim of the Year. Doesn't matter in the eternal scheme of things. God invites us to an eternity of joy. The transitory and perhaps quite difficult nature of our circumstances only further highlights God's incredible offer to us. Looking to eternal life with God isn't a cop-out or crutch for those facing great challenges – it's the answer to why we all experience suffering sooner or later: adversity focuses us on the eternal joy of life with God. Adversity also strengthens our faith and stimulates growth toward moral perfection (James 1.2-4).

So whatever our circumstances God both invites us to an eternity of joy with him and has destroyed the only thing blocking us, sin. That alone should fuel an eternity of rejoicing and thanksgiving. Especially if we live in the West where our lives are probably packed at least with *good things* if not *good relationships*. We realize how many blessings we have once we stop feeling like we

---

Dad's Death

As I complete the writing of this book, I grieve the loss of my father who died just ten days ago. My relationship with dad went from pretty good to nearly ideal during the sixteen months he battled cancer. There's no room for anger at the premature loss of my father - only gratitude to God over the incredible gift he was to us.

"deserve" a bigger house, a better job, a car that doesn't break down, kids that don't cry, etc. The key to gratitude is treating every good thing or relationship as a gift (again, start your list with the items discussed in the above paragraphs). Don't dwell on gifts that haven't been given or are provided only temporarily.

Helps in Thanksgiving

I will give thanks to the Lord with my whole heart . . . I will be glad and exult in you.

Psalm 9.1

Especially if you haven't done much by way of thanksgiving prayer, I suggest simply listing out the many ways God blesses you. The following is a guide for preparing such a thanksgiving list:

1. Start with being made in God's image and likeness. No, start with existing at all (and continuing to exist at this moment)! Being made like him has most to do with the capacities for self awareness, for recognizing goodness, truth and beauty (and their opposites), for the deep joy related to truth, goodness and beauty and much less to do with our physical and intellectual abilities (or lack thereof).
2. Having a personal relationship with God.
3. God's work in establishing that relationship through the death of Jesus and giving us the Holy Spirit.
4. Our families.
5. Our relationships, particularly with fellow believers.
6. Our material provisions and physical and mental gifts.
7. Blessings particular to our life.

Now take some time to create your own thanksgiving list:

❖ _____

❖ _____

❖ _____

❖ _____

❖ _____

❖ _____

❖ _____

❖ _____

❖ _____

Living the Life of Prayer

1. What are your reasons for making time for daily prayer and Scripture reading?

_____

_____

_____

_____

_____

2. Describe a particular blessing in your life.

_____

_____

_____

_____

_____

Action Items

☐ Prayer/scripture reading of _____ minutes per day
☐ Pray for group member: _____ regarding: _____
☐ Pray through your thanksgiving list 3 times

Lesson 7 - Interceding for the Kingdom of God

Rejoice always, **pray constantly,** *give thanks in all circumstances; for this is the will of God in Christ Jesus for you*   I Thessalonians 5.16-18

"Prayer" generally refers to communicating with God in general, but also more narrowly means to petition or intercede. Intercession, like contemplation and thanksgiving, involves accessing God's presence both to be heard but also to learn what God wants to happen. In fact, we should intercede only for what we think or know God wishes or wills[14]. We don't just intercede as "free lancers" or "independent contractors," but as priests of the most high God – not in the *persona Christi* (the person of Christ) as an ordained priest does while celebrating the sacraments – but by virtue of being a member of God's people, which as a group is a royal priesthood and a holy nation[15]. The power of our intercessory prayer comes directly from being part of the body of Christ – the ultimate high priest. As we saw earlier, God weeps and rejoices over whether or not people choose to embrace the fullness of his life and plan for them. As intercessors, we stand with God and pray for God's will for various situations and people. As we behold God's face we also most clearly see his will. While contemplation is our response to God's beauty and glory, and thanksgiving to his goodness to us, intercession is our response to his love for others.

Our heavenly father loves us and wants to give us good things!!!! Ask him for your needs and for good things.[16]   Above all, pray for God's will to be done, which in the long run is always for the best.

Seeking God's will and simply listening for his voice is an important area of prayer in its own right. Ask God questions! Oh Lord, what job do you wish me to have? What do you wish to teach me in this difficult situation? . . . And don't just ask, but also listen. Sometimes God will want us to use our own judgment to figure things out; other times he may himself speak to us quite clearly. When I was considering what to do after graduating from college, I had several options that made sense in human terms but I felt a strong conviction that God wanted me to live in a particular city, which ruled out all options but one!

> **Lord, Teach us to Pray . . .**
>
> *Our Father, who art in heaven,*
>
> 1 *Hallowed be thy name*
> 2 *Thy kingdom come*
> 3 *Thy will be done, on earth as it is in heaven*
>
> 4 *Give us this day our daily bread*
> 5 *And forgive us our trespasses as we forgive those who trespass against us*
> 6 *Lead us not into temptation*
> 7 *But deliver us from evil*

Another major area of intercession is actually asking God to make us like himself. This may be called *transformational prayer*, the substance of which will be considered later in the section on Transformation, lessons 17-24.

I know this all sounds a bit grandiose and ethereal. In practice, however, prayer is rather earthy until we gain heaven. Our lives are fraught with distractions and disorders, hardships and interruptions. Yet, despite all the difficulties of making prayer happen on a daily basis, we can possess no greater joy than simply being with God. Being with God is what we are made for. When we are with God, we do things like contemplate his beauty and glory, rejoice and give thanks over his many blessings to us, and participate in his active love for others. Thank God - otherwise, prayer wouldn't be worth all the bother.

Pray for People

Concerning intercession, the first step is seeking God for his will and purposes regarding our needs, people we care for, and other matters related to the material and spiritual condition of those around us. Even without any advanced discernment, we can be pretty sure that God wants everyone to come into the joy of a relationship with himself and other people and to satisfy all of their material needs. In fact, examine Luke 11.5-13. What does the Lord expect his disciples to pray for? Why?

> ### *Intercession in Amsterdam*
>
> That morning, I happened to be scanning for new radio stations when I came across a talk show promotion of a "Big Sex" sweepstakes for a five day all-expense paid trip to the red-light district of Amsterdam. This shocking promo was still ringing in my ears when Steve – an old friend and business associate - looked at me confidentially and said, "I've got to tell you what happened *to me* in Amsterdam." We had been talking about Christianity, which Steve stopped practicing in childhood, and I dreaded some unseemly revelation.
>
> With nothing to read one night while there on business boredom led Steve to play a "fan and stop" game. Finding a Bible tucked away in a desk, Steve fanned its pages and plopped his finger down in the middle of the page he opened to – right on his own name!
>
> The one in a million odds got his attention. The shock lasted for days and Steve eventually told a work associate. Steve's even greater shock was learning this man had been praying daily for God to reveal himself to Steve!

_____

_____

_____

_____

Helps in Intercession

Beyond a few generalities, there are no ready-made checklists for intercession. Primarily think about and list what is best for yourself and other people *from God's perspective*. I suggest keeping a notebook or prayer journal for this purpose (or pda or word file). For starters prepare a list in the following space:

Person   Petition

❖ _____   _____

❖ _____   _____

❖ _____   _____

❖ _____   _____

❖ _____   _____

❖ _____   _____

❖ _____   _____

As you pray through this list, ask God to reveal his will more fully even as you ask him to act for the benefit of the persons on the list.

A simple formula for intercessory prayer? Open (or close) your time of intercession with the Our Father. Then pray through your list. Set aside several times a week to go through the whole list. You will be surprised at how quickly your list grows into a page or two. You will also be surprised at how God answers your prayers. Close with a Hail Mary.

Many people who pray the rosary use it as a way of interceding. In particular, state your intentions in a prayer before you begin the rosary, for example, "Oh Heavenly King, I ask for such and such . . . Mary, I ask you to intercede to the Father for these matters." Then be mindful of particular intentions while you recite the meditative prayers of the rosary.

> **Hail Mary,**
>
> *Full of grace.*
> *The Lord is with the, blessed are thou among women*
> *and blessed is the fruit of thy womb, Jesus.*
>
> *Holy Mary, Mother of God,*
> *pray for us sinners, now and at the hour of our death.*

Remember, you are not piling up prayers[17] or just performing some duty in praying the rosary, but entering into a rhythm of meditative and intercessory prayer[18].

Living the Life of Prayer

1. What would you have to change in your schedule to pray or read Scripture for 15-30 minutes per day (or to make it to daily Mass)?*

   _____

   _____

   _____

   _____

   _____

   you may notice a certain amount of repetition in the discussion questions in this section - yes, this repetition is deliberate!

2. Have each person in your group pray an intention out loud, e.g., "Lord, we pray that Jane and Paul's marriage would be restored." Then allow a minute or two for the other people to repeat the prayer in their own words, either silently or out loud.

   _____

   _____

   _____

   _____

   _____

Action Items

- ☐ Prayer/scripture reading of _____ minutes per day
- ☐ Pray for group member: _____ regarding: _____
- ☐ Pray through your intercession list 3 times

Lesson 8 – Getting Started

*But when you pray,
go into your room and shut the door and
pray to your Father who is in secret;
and your Father who sees in secret will
reward you.
And in praying do not heap up empty
phrases as the Gentiles do;
for they think that they will be heard for
their many words.*

Matthew 6.6-7

So what are the practical steps involved in experiencing God more deeply in prayer? We actually identified several absolutely crucial steps in the very first lesson in Part III, including simplifying our life. The bottom line is worth reiterating:

> *If we haven't simplified our life enough to have a daily prayer time and attend Mass every Sunday, Jesus isn't Lord of our life and we are hardly his disciple.*

Maintaining holiness is another crucial step from that lesson. After urging you to just start praying daily (if you haven't already), this lesson briefly considers prayer styles and the use of Scripture in prayer. The next two lessons help you chart out your prayer time and develop an action plan for daily and weekly prayer.

Just Do It!

What's the basis for a good prayer life? Not talking about it, not reading about it, not thinking about it, but doing it – and doing it regularly. If you want a good prayer life – don't just go on a retreat or read a book – start praying on a daily basis for fifteen minutes. Realistically, you may need to start with five or ten minutes per day. Start with a minimum that you can manage every day.

Did I already mention the need to actually pray? To pray daily? *My advice is to give up on personal prayer unless it becomes your #1 daily priority.* Otherwise, the press of daily life will quickly dissolve our prayer life into a good intention soon forgotten! The reality is that spending time with the Lord every day is our greatest gift and privilege, not just our Lord's command. Did I already mention that being with God is the ultimate source of joy and happiness? The Lord guarantees that everything will work out fine – actually, as well as it can – if we spend time daily with him. It doesn't matter how pressed we are by the demands of our life (although maybe some of our priorities need to be adjusted). Of course, we must be responsible to our family, job or studies, health, etc. I promise you that God ultimately works everything out way better than we can begin to imagine if we make prayer our top daily priority.

Mary's Choice. See Luke 10.38-42 for the story of Mary & Martha. What does Mary choose for?

_____

_____

Why does Jesus praise this choice?

_____

_____

_____

Methods of Personal Prayer

Just as we have different personalities, we also have different spiritual temperaments[19]. Some of us will do well by singing and speaking to God out loud. Others will find silent prayer best. Some find the Liturgy of the Hours a very fruitful form of prayer. Others write out their prayers in prayer journals. Most find at least some regular reading and meditation on God's Word in one form or another indispensable. Some memorize Scriptures, others find Eucharistic Adoration very powerful, and some combine both! All the varieties of personal prayer are not easily listed.

Most people with a regular personal prayer life rely on several different forms or methods of personal prayer. The trick is finding out which work best for you, and, then, of course, actually using them on a daily basis! Whatever methods and patterns you choose, our daily and weekly rhythm should include large portions of thanksgiving, intercession and contemplation. You should also be mindful in exploring prayer styles that "there is no other way of Christian prayer than Christ. . . . [our prayer] has access to the Father only if we pray 'in the name' of Jesus"[20].

Whatever your prayer method, I can't emphasize enough asking God to reveal himself and develop your relationship with him. Ask God to pour out his Holy Spirit upon you. In imitation of many holy people I have known and because of its success, daily I pray for more of the Holy Spirit:

> *Come Holy Spirit,*
> *Fill the hearts of the faithful.*
> *Enkindle in us the fire of your love.*
> *Be with me all day! Help me to be holy and loving.*

The Word of God in Prayer

Let the Word of Christ dwell in you richly   Colossians 3.16

Scripture has a special role in almost all forms of prayer. God speaks to us through the Bible. The Bible's caretaker, the Church, urges it upon us forcefully![21]. Justly famous is the saying of St. Jerome, a father of the early church:

Ignorance of Scripture is *Ignorance of Christ*.

The Bible is *designed* for use in all aspects of our prayer life. The Psalms, in particular, are the preeminent Christian prayer book[22]. Use the Psalms for thanksgiving, intercession and contemplation. Worship God by praying passages such as the Song of Moses (Exodus 15) and the Canticles of Mary and Zechariah (Luke 1). Meditating on Scripture allows the word of God to work in us (I Thess 2.13), to make its home in us (I John 2.14), and to help purify our hearts (Hebrews 4.12). God speaks to us and feeds us through Scripture reading[23].

I recall shortly after my faith awakening as a freshman in college opening my bible after a late evening of study and finding the words of Scripture coming alive to me. It was Jesus speaking *to me* in the parables. The powerful unfolding and richness of the life of the early church recounted in the Acts of the Apostles was the most riveting of dramas. I even found the story of creation compelling! Sure, I had read these passages before but without the eyes of enlivened faith.

Your Guarantee

Our daily prayer time is essentially the birthright of every Christian: God gives us this time with himself regardless of how demanding and busy our lives are. Sort of like a "free pass" for daily prayer – God guarantees that we will never get "penalized" for praying fifteen minutes a day!

Living the Life of Prayer

1. What are your greatest obstacles to daily prayer? How can you overcome these?

   _____

   _____

   _____

   _____

2. What kinds of prayer are you most comfortable with? What types of prayer would like to explore? Why?

   _____

   _____

   _____

   _____

Action Items

- ☐ Prayer/scripture reading of _____ minutes per day
- ☐ Pray for group member: _____ regarding: _____
- ☐ Memorize Colossians 3.16

Lesson 9 - Charting a Course

This lesson helps you plan out your personal prayer time. If you already are praying on a daily basis, skip to the next section, the "Seasoned Sailor's Boat."

The Beginner's Boat

We are in one of two boats. Some of us are in the beginners' boat where the primary prayers in the past have been the SOS variety – hollering for help when we are about to drown (which may be one of the reasons why God permits adversity in the first place!). I suggest that beginners spend a lot of their initial prayer times simply asking God to reveal himself more and more to you. Meditate on the basic truths of our faith discussed in the earlier lessons.

If you are in the beginners' boat, start with the following recipe, then experiment and vary it over time as you find ways of praying that best suit you.

1. Daily Prayer
   a. Begin by reciting a favorite psalm or passage from the bible (perhaps one from this study).
   b. Spend 5-10 minutes in **Thanksgiving** to God for his goodness to you, praying through your thanksgiving list developed in Lesson 5.
   c. Spend 5-10 minutes of considering God's beauty and glory (**Contemplation**).
      i. Think comparatively about some of the things you described as beautiful above. As an example, "God, you are more beautiful than a sunset on the ocean" or "Your love is far richer than that of my own parents." You could also recite favorite psalms.
      ii. Another strategy is to praise the different attributes of God: "Oh God, you are full of mercy"; "Oh God, you are so loving."
      iii. Whatever you verbalize should be done very slowly . . . let the words hang in the air.
      iv. It often helps to imagine heaven or simply what Jesus is like. We don't "imagine" our relationship with God; rather, we put ourselves in a frame of mind to meet God. You will continue praying because God indeed will fill you himself, with a joy that is indescribable and makes you *know* the completeness and reality of simply being with God.
   d. Spend 5-10 minutes **Interceding**.
      i. As you start out, a large proportion of your prayer time will be devoted to asking God to change your life and fill you more and more with his Holy Spirit - starting with establishing a personal prayer time! Praying for God's power to be at work in

us must become a basic habit of life, ideally prayed nearly as often as we breath, permeating our days rather than merely beginning our designated "prayer time." The fruit of this prayer, coupled with surrendering our will to God, is the transformation in Christ described in Part II of this book as well as power to love others as God loves us.

    ii. Pray through your intercession list developed in Lesson 5.

2. Scripture Reading/Study Every Third Day (or so)
    a. Begin with 5 minutes of prayer (e.g., follow b-c above)
    b. Spend 10-25 minutes reading, studying and meditating on Scripture.
        i. Begin with the gospel of Luke and continue with the Acts of the Apostles.
        ii. Continue with following the readings that are used for Sunday Masses (and daily, if time permits).

3. In addition to Sunday Mass, attend daily Mass once during the week instead of taking a personal prayer time[24].

The Seasoned Sailor's Boat

If you have the good fortune of praying regularly, you might evaluate your prayer time along the following lines:

1. Questions of Consistency
    a. Are you praying at least 15 minutes per day? Pray about whether God wants you to expand that time to 30 minutes or more.
    b. Are you asking God for the Holy Spirit to come down on you daily?

2. Questions of Focus
    a. Is your main, overarching objective in prayer simply to be with God? (Think about it, there are many other worthwhile, but lesser, objectives for prayer.)
    b. Whatever your particular habits or forms of prayer, over the course of the week are you spending substantial time giving thanks, interceding, and contemplating? What about "transformative prayer"? (see Lesson 7 above)
    c. How much Scripture are you reading each week? Do you have a general study and reading plan?

Living the Life of Prayer

1. Describe your experience of daily prayer over the last several months.

_____

_____

_____

_____

_____

2. What challenges have you experienced in praying on a daily basis? How did you overcome them?

_____

_____

_____

_____

_____

Action Items

☐ Prayer/scripture reading of _____ minutes per day

☐ Pray for group member: _____ regarding: _____

☐ Decide which boat you are in and evaluate your prayer time accordingly

---

Lesson 10 – Action Plan for Personal Prayer

Mary, Albrecht Dürer

Set Some Goals

How much time to pray? Your goal will vary according to your particular situation. Most people might eventually build up to ½ hour per day of prayer or more, perhaps starting out with only five or ten minutes. John Paul II spent one hour in personal prayer in addition to praying a set of psalms and related prayers (the Liturgy of the Hours) and celebrating Mass every day. Many people find that first thing in the morning is the best time for prayer. Making room for prayer may require listing and analyzing your priorities. If prayer is your number one priority, which lesser priorities must yield time to daily prayer? Where is the best place in your daily and weekly schedule to fit in prayer? Have you ever laid out for yourself a daily schedule? Like with most things, go ahead and explicitly ask God for help. Ask God to free up the time for prayer and simply to get you started.

> **Once you're tucked in?**
>
> A good friend of mine shared that his best time for daily prayer "is when I get really comfortable, right before bed. In fact, I get in bed and shut my eyes. Its automatic. I can't imagine not praying at that time." Just as I was mentally rescheduling my daily prayer to so desirable a time slot, my friend added, "the only problem is, I only pray for two minutes before falling asleep."

So, what's it going to be for you? Take five minutes right now to consider a daily prayer time. How much does God want you to pray? What parts of the day work best for prayer? What is a sustainable prayer time on a daily basis – five minutes? Fifteen minutes? One-half hour? Where is the best place for prayer? Your bedroom? Your office/study cubicle? Taking a walk? A chapel? Ask God to give you wisdom and direction in setting the following goals:

Time for daily prayer: _____ (minimum)

to _____ (target)

Location: _____ (preferred spot)

_____ (backup spot)

When: _____ (preferred time)

_____ (backup time)

Your Prayer Time

Indicate below the pattern of prayer you are shooting for by filling in the blanks.

Sample

	MON	TUES	WED	THURS	FRI	SAT	SUN
TYPE	Prayer	Prayer	Mass	Prayer	Scripture	Prayer	Mass
PLACE	Den	Den	St. Paul	Den	Den	Starbucks	St. Rita
TIME	7 am	7 am	Noon	7 am	7 am	8 am	11 am
DURATION	:15	:15	:40	:15	:20	:30	1:15
BACKUP TIME	10 pm	10 pm	10 pm	10 pm	?	?	n/a

Yours

	MON	TUES	WED	THURS	FRI	SAT	SUN
TYPE							
PLACE							
TIME							
DURATION							
BACKUP TIME							

Keep in mind that your schedule will change from time to time and you will need to adjust the above plan. You may wish to cut this out and paste it on your mirror or some other place; or keep it in your wallet as a reminder. You can download blank forms from www.GodsPlanForYourLife.org or simply write out your own.

Accountability

New Year's resolutions are quickly forgotten. An excellent way to boost our success in reaching our prayer goals is to make ourselves accountable. In high school football, by joining the team you make yourself accountable to the coach to make the practices and to work hard. The coach challenges and pushes you to be successful, offering praise and encouragement. You are ashamed to run wind sprints at a trot.

Make yourself accountable to your men's group to make your prayer goals. Encourage each other. Challenge each other. Of course, making ourselves accountable to each other is simply harnessing a natural force. We don't like to fail. Having to admit failure to others can be a powerful incentive to hit our goals. While accountability may help you to get in the habit of praying, never lose sight of the real reason for prayer: simply being with God.

Living the Life of Prayer

Want to die . . . spiritually and eternally? Read John 4.10-15 and John 7.37-39. What do you think Jesus means by living water? How does this apply *to you*?

_____

_____

_____

_____

Why does Jesus compare prayer to going to the well in a desert society without plumbing?

_____

_____

_____

_____

Action Items

☐   Prayer/scripture reading of _____ minutes per day

☐   Pray for group member: _____ regarding: _____

☐   Call one of the guys in your group this week and ask him how prayer is going

---

—— Equipping for Battle ——

Lesson 11 – What's Stopping Us?

Consider St. Paul's description of life prior to having a relationship with Christ, when we were "spiritually" dead:

> *You he made alive, when you were dead through the trespasses and sins in which you once walked, following the course of this **world**, following the **prince of the power of the air**, the spirit that is now at work in the sons of disobedience. Among these we all once lived in the passions of our **flesh**, following the desires of body and mind, and so we were by nature children of wrath, like the rest of mankind.*
>
> Ephesians 2.1-3

Most of the New Testament writers discuss the world, the flesh and the Devil (the "prince of the power of the air") as three forces that undermine our being with God, let alone becoming like Jesus and loving whom he loves. As Christians, we must contend against these forces throughout our life on earth. Let's take a closer look.

The World

The "world" is used in Scripture in two distinct senses. The first sense is morally neutral and refers to all human beings, as in "For God so loved the world, that he gave his only son" (John 3.16). The second sense in which "world" is used in Scripture has clearly negative connotations, referring to the society and culture – and especially its embedded values – of all those who have not accepted God's plan for their lives, as in John's admonition to love not the "world" (I John 2.15).

The fact is that almost everyone who hasn't accepted God's plan for their lives has one of their own. While these plans may involve pursuing good things, they often do so in a warped or exaggerated way, one which ultimately distorts us and undermines our happiness. Consider consumerism, i.e., a hyper-emphasis on acquiring consumer goods. We all know people subtly (or not so subtly) dominated by the desire to have

> **Love not the World**
>
> Do not love the world or the things in the world. If any one loves the world, love for the Father is not in him. I John 2:15

a big house, car, vacations, etc. Since only God is capable of filling us with true joy and happiness, pursuing anything else dooms us to trying futilely to draw joy out of dry holes or putrid wells. Sex is another example. God imbues sex with a certain often rather wonderful pleasure, but sex fails to quench our appetite. So if you don't know any better (and perhaps even if you do) – a fixation on sex turns your spouse into an object of gratification undermining intimacy and friendship. Or how easily can our quest for sexual gratification lead to lying or manipulating another person, whether we are married or single?

Or consider developing a child's potential. While it's wonderful to see your child cultivate their gifts and accomplish much, how easily can such efforts undermine the time you actually spend relating to them and create in them a mindset wedding happiness to accomplishments? Or take work, leisure, one's appearance, or, just about any good thing. Sometimes when people fail to wrench satisfaction out of good things, they try evil ones. The world has all kinds of ideas and plans for making us happy – all of which are doomed to failure.

Application Question #1 - In what specific areas have you most experienced the world's influence?

_____

_____

_____

_____

The "Flesh"

To make matters worse, our own sins and those of others affect us even after we repent! Sin deforms and destroys who we

> *True Story*
>
> The glee and joy of kindergartners is infectious. You're part of the game, no questions asked, tumbling from one delight to the next. "But what happens by the time they reach middle school?" wondered the young seminarian helping out as a grade school gym teacher. "The bright faces had mostly grown long for my eighth graders. The world, the flesh and the devil have a way of beating us up and stealing our joy."

are – and we have all sinned. The damage of sin often takes a while for God's grace to restore. Much of the damage is to our power to choose. Since God makes us free, he provides help only as we ask: failing to ask makes it infinitely more difficult to receive his help. Our old habits of choosing poorly (sinning) are often called "the flesh" or "the old man" in Scripture. Impatience sometimes frothing over into temper loss is probably my own biggest ongoing struggle against the flesh. Read Galatians 5.13-26. How does Paul describe the influence of the "flesh" [25]?

_____

_____

_____

_____

If you wish to be with God, you must allow him to transform you by living by his Spirit. Notice how deadly the works of the flesh can be in v. 21?

Application Question #2 - What areas of the flesh do you struggle with most?

_____

_____

_____

_____

Action Items

☐   Prayer/scripture reading of _____ minutes per day
☐   Pray for group member: _____ regarding: _____
☐   Keep an eye out for the world's influences in your life

The World and the Devil: What Catholics Believe

408 The consequences of original sin and of all men's personal sins put the world as a whole in the sinful condition aptly described in St. John's expression, "the sin of the world." This expression can also refer to the negative influence exerted on people by communal situations and social structures that are the fruit of men's sins.

409 This dramatic situation of "the whole world [which] is in the power of the evil one" (I John 5:19; cf. I Peter 5.8) makes man's life a battle:

> The whole of man's history has been the story of dour combat with the powers of evil, stretching, so our Lord tells us, from the very dawn of history until the last day. Finding himself in the midst of the battlefield man has to struggle to do what is right, and it is at great cost to himself, and aided by God's grace,
> that he succeeds in achieving his own inner integrity. (Vatican II, *Gaudium et Spes*, 37 §2).

2852 "A murderer from the beginning, . . . a liar and the father of lies," Satan is "the deceiver of the whole world."

Catechism of the Catholic Church

Lesson 12 – What Else Is Stopping Us?

For we are not contending against flesh and blood, but against the principalities, against the powers, against the world rulers of this present darkness, against the spiritual hosts of wickedness in the heavenly places.

Ephesians 6.12

The Devil

To make matters even worse, in addition to human beings the "world" includes spiritual powers and angels, who pursue their own plans for being happy. Unfortunately, those who reject God's plan generally fall prey to an age-old happiness substitute: dominating others! Scripture refers to the king of these would-be rulers as Satan. Consider Jesus' experience in Luke 4.1-13.

Over whom does Satan rule? Do you think Satan exerts the same power today?

_____

_____

_____

_____

Does Satan give up after Jesus resists his first temptation? What should that teach us?

_____

_____

_____

In John 13.2 and 14.30, we see that Satan keeps an eye on things and swayed Judas into betraying Jesus into the crucifixion. Check out Gibson's *The Passion of the Christ* for an interpretation of Satan's role in trying to destroy Jesus. Or attend your parish's Holy Thursday and Good Friday liturgies.

Don't believe in evil spirits today? Consider the twenty-plus million who died of genocide in the last century. Look at the work of Al Qaeda. Better still, look at how many little suggestions you experience to be nasty, lust after money, etc. Ever get really scared?

Among the many forces driving our culture, Catholics believe a significant force strives to undermine God's plans for our lives:

> Satan or the devil and the other demons are fallen angels who have freely refused to serve God and his plan. Their choice against God is definitive. They try to associate man in their revolt against God.   CCC 414

In fact, the Church understands that the last petition of the Our Father is specifically directed against this enemy to God's plans:

> In this petition, evil is not an abstraction, but refers to a person, Satan, the Evil One, the angel who opposes God. The devil (*dia-bolos*) is the one who "throws himself across" God's plan and his work of salvation accomplished in Christ.
>
> CCC 2851

Scripture and Catholic teaching often refers to the influence of Satan and the negative influence of the fruit of men's sin in culture and society as the influence of the *World*. You cannot just say "the Devil made me do it"; the point rather is that a Catholic disciple of Christ must carefully examine whether his life corresponds more to God's plan or to his own plan or the world's.

Fear Not!

Are not five sparrows sold for two pennies? And not one of them is forgotten before God. Why, even the hairs of your head are all numbered. Fear not; you are of more value than many sparrows . . . Fear not, little flock, for it is your Father's good pleasure to give you the kingdom.

Luke 12.6-7,32

Our Response

A full consideration of all the ways God wants us to repel the World, the Flesh and the Devil is beyond the scope of this book[26]. In brief, the general response is:

- Reject the passions and desires of the flesh as providing only fleeting and hollow pleasure, destructive of how and for what God made you (Galatians 5.24)
- Reject the World's deceptive plans for our happiness and embrace God's (Ephesians 1.3-14)
- Put on the whole armor of God against the wiles of the Devil . . . through faith, the Word of God, and prayer (Ephesians 6). Translation: constantly remember God's love for us and our salvation in Christ.

The bigger picture is to embrace fully God's plan for our life. The key to embracing God's plan on a daily basis? Calling on God's power, which we will consider next.

Discussion Questions

Application Question #1– Describe where you have personally observed the Evil One at work or where you believe his hand is at work in society.

_____

_____

_____

_____

Application Question #2– In what ways does society tend to "pooh pooh" supernatural forces or deny their existence?

_____

_____

_____

_____

Action Items

- ☐ Prayer/scripture reading of _____ minutes per day
- ☐ Pray for group member: _____ regarding: _____
- ☐ Meditate on the Catechism and Scripture references in this lesson

Lesson 13 –
Our Power Source

St. Peter's Basilica, Bernini

Rekindle the gift of God that is within you through the laying on
of hands [baptism and confirmation] . . . a spirit of power and love and self control.

I Timothy 1.6-7

Christianity is no self-improvement program! Rather, it's a letting-God-transform-me-by-his-Power program. You don't pay for it with bucks (at least directly). We pay for it by laying down our life, taking up our cross and taking Jesus as our Lord. The improvements are eternal, not ephemeral. Rather than growing self-confident, we grow into the stature required to be an intimate friend of the most powerful, awe-inspiring being in the universe. Rather than gaining wealth, we become heirs to the Kingdom of Everything. Rather than learning how to win friends and influence people, a radiance of love, joy, and humility proves irresistible to those around us. Rather than supercharging our career, physique, and love life – whatever – we prepare ourselves for an eternity of joy.

When you think about it, the promises of Christianity do boggle the mind – the promises of becoming like Christ are so outrageous that advertising them probably should be outlawed! We're supposed to look like Christ, the image of the invisible God, as it says in Colossians 1? Despite the world, the flesh and the Devil? In reality, these claims are all so much hot air unless you tap into the Holy Spirit, "[who] restores to the baptized the divine likeness lost through sin" and "makes us act out of love"[27].

The Power Plant

Consider how the following passages apply to your life; how can you respond practically to each?

John 15.4-5

_____

_____

Ephesians 1.19 & 3.20

_____

_____

_____

Galatians 2.20

_____

_____

_____

II Corinthians 12.9-10

_____

_____

_____

Now we are asking the big questions! So how do we _abide_ with Jesus? You may be able to guess the answer. In John we see Jesus identify the Eucharist as a way of abiding in him (John 6.56). Take another look at the quote opening this lesson. John also speaks about this power in John 7.37-39. What is another way of tapping into God's power?

_____

_____

_____

Spiritually Connected

How can the Holy Spirit be our life if our heart is far from him?

CCC 2744

We access God's power – the gift of the Holy Spirit – by asking for it. Grace is God's power to make us holy and to use us in evangelism and to help the Church grow.[28] It is a gift of the Holy Spirit. Like the Samaritan women who lived in a dry land and had to fetch water every day for their survival, we need to drink of the Holy Spirit _daily_ if not _hourly_ to survive and flourish (see John 4 and 7.37-39). We access God's power through our regular daily prayer time as well as through the sacraments of the Church; for good reason is the Church called the Temple of the Holy Spirit. We power our electrical appliances by continuously connecting to the electrical utility. Similarly, God powers lives of holiness and love by the Holy Spirit.

> **_Cardinal Suenens on Toasters_**
>
> Cardinal Suenens, one of the architects of Vatican II, once said that the Christian life is like a toaster: it doesn't work unless you plug it in. You plug it in by receiving the Holy Spirit.

Prayer is how we connect to God's power grid. Fasting can amp up prayer.[29] Stay connected throughout the day by praying constantly. Make staying connected to God a higher priority than staying connected to news, family, friends, and work associates through cell phones, email and the web. Make your prayers very specific.

Discussion Questions

1. Do you find it challenging to ask for God's help all the time? Why or why not? What might help?

   _____

   _____

   _____

2. What needs to change in your life for your prayer and sacramental life to become your top priorities?

   _____

   _____

Action Items

□ Prayer/scripture reading of _____ minutes per day

□ Pray for group member: _____ regarding: _____

□ Memorize one of the Scripture passages at the beginning of this lesson

---

ADDENDUM

Lifetime Quest? Dealing with Legacy Sin

While daily or hourly prayer fuels our transformation, how many days or years will it take? When will we become saints? The answer ultimately depends on how fully we give ourselves over to God's plan for our life, and to some degree, on overcoming the residual damage of our sins and those of others.

As society veers further from God's plans, unless we were still more deliberate and energetic in pursuing God's plan, our lives likely reflect damage from the "world" – which often can be rather ugly. For example, something like half of those counting themselves Christian men in the U.S. have serious pornography, masturbation or other sexual addictions. Many of us are scarred emotionally from divorce or abuse. Extramarital sex and broken relationships may seriously undermine our ability to form permanent marital relationships or trust our spouses; like society, we come to view our partner mainly through sexual eyes. Society's intense pre-occupation with physical, academic, and professional achievement may deeply distort ones self image. Enslavement to greed, pride, and fear encloses us in ourselves, isolating us from God and other people and damaging those around us. Craving love and attention from fellow human beings who are themselves increasingly self-absorbed contributes to a variety of emotional illnesses, such as eating disorders. Dysfunctional and disordered families and the world's hyper-emphasis on sexual fulfillment – in addition to the above factors – help fuel same-sex attractions.

Sin and wounded-ness do have a way of multiplying in a person's life. In fact, sin can "infect" or exacerbate any pre-existing wounded-ness. In a society that glorifies vice and sneers at God's plans, the multiplication and corresponding damage is often exponential. The ways in which we have been damaged by our own sins and shortcomings – and by those of others – can be called "legacy sin." One definition of legacy is:

> Something handed down from an ancestor or a predecessor or from the past.[30]

In the case of legacy sin, what is handed down is from our own "past" involving our own or others' sins and shortcomings. For example, there may be a pattern of criticism which our parents picked up from, and were subjected to by, our grandparents and perhaps even our great grandparents. When we in turn grow up in a home permeated by criticism we are both wounded by that criticism and often begin to practice it ourselves. Thus, before we can come to experience God's love, we may need to be healed from that wound and sin of criticism. Some of our parents lacked—to varying degrees—the ability to love us well, to provide for our emotional and spiritual needs. This deficit produces deep wounds, especially in infants and young children. These wounds, in turn, can affect our capacity both to experience God's love and to live out what he commands.

But we need not remain stuck in our wounded-ness and patterns of sin. For Christ came precisely to "preach the Good News to the poor" - which is especially those of us who are weak, wounded, addicted, emotionally distressed, etc. Furthermore, he said "I have come to call sinners, not the virtuous." As he draws us to himself, we may see that we need help from others in addressing the wounds and sins of our past or present (such as addiction). God has provided us with many resources to address these problems, including qualified psychologists and other professionals, the sacrament of confession and spiritual direction. A variety of programs and ministries provide specific and general help in healing, such as Marriage Encounter, Retrouvaille, twelve step programs (e.g., AA), etc. Please see www.GodsPlanforYourLife.org for a listing of some of these programs.

Perhaps the most healing reality of all is the Body of Christ—those fellow Christians who are emotionally healthy and can nurture and love us into being the person God intended us to be. Spend time with loving people transformed by Christ, and you will begin to experience the love of God, which is the most powerful healer of all.

Lesson 14 – Fighting the Good Fight: Our Effort

Work out your own salvation with fear and trembling;
for God is at work in you, both to will and to work for his good pleasure.

Not that I have already obtained this or am already perfect; but I press on . . .
forgetting what lies behind and straining forward to what lies ahead, I press on
toward the goal for the prize of the upward call of God in Christ Jesus.

Philippians 2.12-13; 3.12-14

It is true that God forgives us and makes us holy and charitable *by his power*, but only to the extent we ask his forgiveness and join our will to his. This *joining our will to his* is where the rub comes in. We may be convinced that our highest joy and happiness is found precisely in becoming like Christ and loving others, but the process of such transformation and the living of a life of charity may be hard, at least at first, and is always costly. Look at our master: Jesus came to serve others at the cost of strenuous daily effort and ultimately supreme humiliation and pain. Like our master, embracing the Father's will for us requires strenuous daily effort, although only a few of us will ever be called to anything like our Lord's sacrifice. All of us must contend with a world generally hostile to God's plan, together with overcoming our own sinful tendencies and our spiritual enemies. However sweet the reward, following the Lord implies taking up our cross and the attitude of a servant – and this takes effort on our part.

Discipleship starts with making Jesus lord of our lives and putting everything aside to follow him (Part I, Lesson 5). Living out his lordship requires three things:

1) Awareness of God's will
2) God's power
3) Our effort

The Spirit of God through Scripture and the Church makes us aware of the common elements of God's will or plan for each of us: being with him and his people, becoming like him, and loving whom he loves - in other words, *conversion, transformation* and *mission*. While God provides the power – grace – to be transformed in holiness and charity and to live out our respective missions, it is up to us to join our efforts[31] to his power in becoming "new creations."

Blessed are those who . . . *show effort*

I have fought the good fight . . . there is reserved for me the crown of righteousness.

II Timothy 4

Blessed are those who hunger and thirst, are persecuted, mourn, make peace . . . think about it: the beatitudes all require effort. As much as the New Testament proclaims God's power at work in us, it also greatly emphasizes the need for our effort: faith without works is dead (James 2). As we considered at the end of Part I, Jesus graphically and personally, as it were, measures the effort required to follow him in terms of taking up a cross of crucifixion on a daily basis. Analogies of striving, conflict, building, war and even self mutilation[32] nail home the effort Jesus expects of us in loving others, from "washing feet" to laying down our lives. The effort is even more radical when we consider how Jesus expands the circle of people whom we are to serve beyond our friends and family (although loving those closest to us can be the greatest challenge!).

Read Luke 10.29-37 and Matthew 5.43-47. Who are the "others" whom we are to love and serve?

_____

_____

_____

Paul translates taking up our cross into the supreme effort of "crucifying our flesh with its passions and desires" and our servanthood as pointing to becoming slaves of one another in love. Paul repeatedly uses the language of soldiering to describe the perseverance and intensity of battle in the Christian life[33]. Consider Paul's instruction on effort to one of his key disciples in II Timothy 2.1-5. What metaphors does Paul use in describing the effort he expects from Timothy?

_____

_____

_____

Being a disciple is not for sissies. In fact, one of the lessons from the Sermon on the Mount in Matthew 5-7 is that no amount of effort on our part will bring us to the perfection of holiness and charity that God requires: being Jesus' disciple is impossible without his power. Yet the Lord expects us to throw everything we've got into this business.

Focus of Our Efforts

Put to death the deeds of the body . . .
Put on the Lord Jesus Christ   Romans 8.13; 13.14

The focus of our efforts to grow as disciples include the following:

1) eliminating sins (vices) and fighting temptations (spiritual warfare)
2) developing habits of being good and loving others (virtues and the fruit of the Spirit)
3) seeking out and embracing God's specific plan for our daily lives

Yet it would be wrong to say that our goals are simply moral improvement and obedience to God. Rather, we are striving to put on Jesus Christ, walk by the Spirit, partake in the divine nature, and receive God's very own Spirit and power for holiness. We have all met "morally correct" people who are lifeless and flat, doing the right things but without warmth or love. Far more alive are people into whose hearts God has poured his very own Spirit; far warmer are those basking in the glow of the Father's tremendous love; utterly irresistible are those whose faces have grown radiant with the beauty and glory of the living God. Indeed, the focus of our efforts transcends (and fulfills) all morality: it is to collaborate in God's work of truly becoming "new creations" after the image of his own son.

The first two of these categories relate to growth in holiness and Christian character and, following the above quote from Romans 8, involve "putting to death the deeds of the body" and "putting on Jesus Christ".[34] The final category of effort – embracing God's plan for our daily lives - is really quite broad, but the following elements apply to everyone:

- ◆ Prayer and Sacramental Life
- ◆ Christian Identity and Worldview
- ◆ Loving and Caring for Others
- ◆ Christian Pattern of Life
- ◆ Strong Family Life
- ◆ Christian Fellowship
- ◆ Life of Mission

Saving further exploration of these elements until later lessons, the next several lessons consider some of the ways in which we can collaborate with God's work. What types of effort can we make in striving for this transformation? We know the Lord requires maximum effort on our part; what does this look like in our day-to-day lives?

Discussion Questions

1. Which do you naturally tend to emphasize more: God's power or our effort? How can this emphasis be a strength?

   _____

   _____

   _____

2. How can your emphasis be a weakness?

   _____

   _____

Action Items

☐ Prayer/scripture reading of _____ minutes per day

☐ Pray for group member: _____ regarding: _____

☐ Focus this week on whichever tends to be weaker: God's power or your effort

---

Lesson 15 – Doing Battle

Types of Effort

Be Serious and Discipline Yourselves   I Peter 4.7

Making Jesus lord of our life requires the effort of laying down our lives and giving them to Christ. This process of dying to ourselves is often one that we must revisit again and again in our Christian lives. It's as if our old flesh has nine *thousand* lives! This act of faith in a small way resembles Jesus' effort in the garden just before his arrest: not my will, but yours be done. The Church in her pastoral wisdom invites us to repeat our baptismal vows every Easter partly in order to re-affirm Jesus' lordship over our lives, the counter-part of which is dying to ourselves. In a certain way, we draw down from the treasury of Jesus' effort of laying down his life every time we receive communion, inasmuch as we participate in his salvific act.

Sometimes our effort is simply to "let go" of our lives. We can so easily clench our lives, like a fist grasping money, that God must wrench them free with great force (with our permission, of course). This wrenching could take the form of literally losing someone or something very dear to us, such as a job, spouse, parent, child, our health, an honor, etc. For some of us, our "effort" may involve our will being broken, in the manner of a trainer breaking in a young horse. The effort is mostly on the part of the trainer; the horse at some point just "lets go of his will." Perhaps our effort in laying down our lives involved the pain of wrenching or of being broken.

Application Question. Describe the effort required in making Jesus Lord of your life.

_____

_____

_____

_____

Don't be surprised if there comes a point where you find yourself back on the throne of your life and need to repeat this process. Perhaps you are in that position now. If so, the best thing to do is to let go of your life (to avoid the pain of being "re-broken" later, if for no other reason) and give your whole life to God, right now, without reservation. Simply pray,

> Oh God, I give my life fully to you without reservation: I am yours. Be lord of my life.
> Take me, hold me, do with me as you see fit.
> In the name of the Father and of the Son and of the Holy Spirit, Amen.

The struggle to give your life to God, itself made possible by his grace, may be your greatest and creates the foundation for discipleship. What efforts are helpful for growing as a disciple? The following chart lists some efforts and associated aspects of discipleship.

We know that prayer and the Eucharist are the foundation of our efforts, being most helpful for all aspects of discipleship. Our prayer life has a pivotal role in our transformation: we must

	TYPE OF EFFORT	PRAYER AND SACRAMENTAL LIFE	CHRISTIAN IDENTITY & WORLDVIEW	HOLINESS & CHRISTIAN CHARACTER – Put to Death Sin	– Put on Christ	– Maintenance & Growth	CHRISTIAN PATTERN OF LIFE	LOVING & CARING FOR OTHERS	STRONG FAMILY LIFE	CHRISTIAN FELLOWSHIP	LIFE OF MISSION
CONVERSION	fear eternal separation from Father (imperfect contrition)			+							
	mourn over our sins and vices			+							
	avoid the near occasion of sin			+		+	+		+		
	hate evil and sin		+	+		+					
	hunger for righteousness		+	+	+	+					+
SACRAMENTAL & DEVOTIONAL	PRAYER AND EUCHARIST (daily)	+	+	+	+	+	+	+	+	+	+
	CONFESSION	+		+	+	+	+		+		
	fear offending the Father (perfect contrition)		+	+	+	+					
	do penance and make reparation			+							
	EXAMINE CONSCIENCE (DAILY)	+	+	+	+	+	+	+	+	+	+
	perform spiritual warfare	+	+	+	+	+			+	+	+
	take Lent as a season of prayer, fasting and almsgiving	+	+	+	+	+	+	+	+		+
	fast (weekly)			+	+	+	+		+		+
	spiritual reading (weekly if not daily)		+	+	+	+	+	+	+		+
GROWTH AND TRANSFORMATION	exercise self-discipline & self-control	+		+	+	+	+	+	+	+	+
	be accountable to, and encouraged by, a faith sharing group	+	+	+	+	+	+	+	+	+	+
	be pure of heart	+	+	+	+	+		+	+	+	+
	be poor in spirit: simplicity of life	+	+	+	+	+	+	+	+	+	+
	be meek: rely on God for our power		+	+	+	+	+	+	+		+
	be humble: see yourself as you are	+	+	+	+	+	+		+	+	+
	focus effort on one virtue or fruit of the Spirit at a time			+	+						
	"train" in the face of adversity and hardship			+	+			+	+	+	+
	be committed & persevere: we are "in it for the long haul"	+		+	+	+		+	+	+	+
	become "slaves" to one another in love			+	+		+	+	+	+	+
	spend ourselves for the kingdom: apostolic suffering			+	+		+		+		+

constantly ask for God's help. Accessing God's power for change through prayer, confession, and the Eucharist cannot be emphasized enough. Some of the types of efforts are really virtues or character traits, which are more precisely habits or dispositions to act. A daily examination of conscience is universally helpful in living for God, which we will consider next.

Discussion Questions

1. What types of effort seem to be most important for your spiritual growth right now? Why?

   _____

   _____

   _____

2. How might these efforts help you grow?

   _____

   _____

   _____

Action Items

- ☐ Prayer/scripture reading of _____ minutes per day
- ☐ Pray for group member: _____ regarding: _____
- ☐ Devote your attention this week to one of the efforts on the chart _____

Lesson 16 - Test Yourself

Examine yourselves to see whether you are living in the faith, test yourselves.

II Corinthians 13.5

Daily Examination of Conscience

A daily examination of conscience is how we measure our efforts in embracing God's plan for our life (among other things). We first form our consciences according to God's law as found in Scripture and Church teaching. Since Jesus is lord of our lives, we must sensitize our consciences to the *imperatives of discipleship*: becoming like Jesus and loving whom God loves – which imperatives, in fact, this book tries to help you apply concretely to your life. A daily examination of conscience considers the following:

- Sin ("violations of holiness")
- Love of God and Neighbor ("life of charity")
- Discipleship Effort

God is going to do everything he can on his part to draw us, woo us, charm us, guide us, shock us, and even frighten us into accepting the magnificent life he has planned out for us, but we have to say yes and seek after him with all our hearts. God provides the power to become holy and loving, yet it takes real effort to take up this new life. Next to daily prayer and the sacraments, examining ourselves every day is the most important discipline for spiritual growth. St. Ignatius, in fact, recommends examining our consciences *twice each day*! So, how do we do it? I recommend the following guidelines[35].

At first, make sure you have properly formed your conscience as to **violations of holiness**, i.e., what offends our all-holy God. Depending on your catechetical background and how much your conscience has been shaped by the world and dulled by patterns of sin, this may take some time. The most complete guide is the *Catechism*, especially the section on the Ten Commandments (paragraphs 2052-2557) and its Index. Lesson 19 briefly discusses the life of holiness. The examination of conscience in the Appendix is a handy reference yet contains only a partial listing of sins. Our response to violations of holiness is repentance, asking God's forgiveness, and, perhaps, making reparation and doing penance. Major violations (grave or mortal sin) also *require* reconciliation through the sacrament of confession. Confession is also *very helpful* in overcoming minor violations (venial sin) and *may be necessary,* inasmuch as venial sins harden into habits and can eventually kill off your life with God.

The **life of charity** is a life of loving God and neighbor (i.e., those around you). The mark of charity towards God is joy, manifested in a continuous and relatively passive manner as cheerfulness and a fundamental disposition of gratitude and awe. Are we actively loving God by obeying him, spending time with him in prayer, and loving others? We love our neighbor by tangibly caring for those around us, starting with our families. The mark of charity towards others is patience, gentleness, esteem, and even tenderness. Charity towards neighbor must be expressed in practical and concrete ways. Remember, we can't love God whom we can't see if we fail to love those around us whom we can see and that faith without works is dead, according to Saints John and James.

Are you really trying? The chart in the last lesson helps us measure our **discipleship effort.** In a certain way, the daily examination of conscience is the parent of all discipleship effort, both as a means of both nurturing and disciplining other efforts. Don't wait to begin a daily examination of conscience until you've got a perfectly formed conscience: start today with what you've got and build from there! I suggest performing your examination in the evening just before bed and keeping it brief, say, three to five minutes, although you may initially and on occasion find spending more time helpful. Remind yourself in the morning of anything that deserves further prayer. Limit your review to the last day and develop a set of examination questions that fit your challenges with sin, the life of charity, and discipleship effort, as well as particular areas of growth such as establishing a prayer time or acquiring a particular virtue. Keep your daily examination simple and do-able; we needn't be as exhaustive as in preparing for confession.

Application Exercise

To get started, develop your own daily examination of conscience by completing the chart below. Consult the Examination of Conscience for Daily Use in the Appendix to help fill out some questions particular to you in each area.

I. Loving God with all our heart, mind and soul
- Have I prayed, read Scripture or gone to Mass today?
- Was my demeanor one of joy, cheerfulness, and gratitude?
- _____
- _____
- _____

II. Loving our neighbor as our self
- Did I cheerfully serve my family, those for whom I am responsible, and my neighbor?
- Have I interceded for those who don't know Christ?
- Was I humble, kind, generous, chaste, and patient with others?
- How did I fail to love others as Christ would have?
- _____
- _____
- _____

III. Keeping the Commandments
- Did I "idolize" some material possession, worldly or spiritual fame, or someone's affection?
- Did I say the Lord's name in anger or carelessly?

- Did I go to Sunday Mass? Did I work needlessly on Sunday?
- _____
- Did I properly care for my parents?
- _____
- Did I harm or sin against anybody?
- _____
- Did I fail to be chaste, i.e., to avoid any form of lust?
- _____
- Was I completely fair in my work and dealings with others?
- _____
- Was I completely honest with everyone?
- _____
- Did I succumb to thoughts of wishing I was married to another person?
- Did I grow frustrated or despair because I am not married?
- _____
- Have I been materialistic or pre-occupied with acquiring something?
- _____

IV. Keeping Church Law
- Have I supported the Church?
- Have I been reverential at Mass, especially by observing the communion fast?
- _____

You can access other examination of conscience templates at www.GodsPlanForYourLife.org.

Discussion Questions

1. What are the primary influences in forming your conscience? Do you feel it's properly formed?

   _____
   _____
   _____

2. What areas of your conscience need further formation?

   _____
   _____

Action Items

☐ Prayer/scripture reading of _____ minutes per day
☐ Pray for group member: _____ regarding: _____
☐ Examine your conscience every night before bed

Transformation
(Becoming Like Jesus)

Michelangelo, Sistine Chapel

Lesson 17 - Being Changed from One Degree of Glory to the Next

Those who love him, who are called according to his purpose . . . he also predestined to be conformed to the image of his Son, in order that he might be the first-born among many brethren.   Romans 8.28-9

It is in Christ, "the image of the invisible God," that man has been created "in the image and likeness" of the Creator. It is in Christ, Redeemer and Savior, that the divine image, disfigured in man by the first sin, has been restored to its original beauty and ennobled by the grace of God. CCC 1701

As we saw in Part I, we gain true and eternal joy from experiencing God's love as well as from beholding him who is ablaze with a love, holiness, and beauty beyond our imagining, both now through prayer and in heaven when we see him face to face. You are made for this joy.

As we draw near to God, he transforms us into his own likeness. The Holy Spirit not only makes us look like him and act like him, but comes to motivate and animate our desires. Chief among these desires are longing simply to be with God and his people and a certain profound pleasure in loving others. Counter-cultural, eh?

> We all, with unveiled face, beholding the glory of the Lord, are being changed into his likeness from one degree of glory to another; for this comes from the Lord who is the Spirit. . . . Therefore, if any one is in Christ, he is a new creation; the old has passed away, behold, the new has come.
>
> II Corinthians 3:18, 5.17

The key ingredient for this transformation on our side, as with gaining a relationship with God and growing in prayer, is that we must ask for it. We must *ask God* to change us – I should say, *get in the habit of asking God* to change us, as it's probably going to take a while! Of course, we also struggle to embrace God's work by deliberately focusing our will, avoiding occasions of sin, practicing virtue whether we enjoy it or not, and generally, as St. Paul says, by *running the race* and *fighting the good fight* until we reach heaven.

The Jerk Problem

As we saw earlier in Part I, change is not optional: we must become perfect as our heavenly father is perfect, holy as he is holy, loving as he is loving. It all sounds a little circular. Basically, God doesn't want to be surrounded by jerks. You and I, to modify a phrase from Alcoholics Anonymous, are *recovering jerks*, more or less (I speak here with much personal authority). Forgiven jerks, but still wanting to do jerky things. So God is going to make us wonderful people both for our sake and his sake (and our collective sakes), because we are going to be with him forever, right?

> Sanctifying grace . . . perfects the soul itself *to enable it to live with God, to act by his love.* CCC 2000

Why prolong your misery? For all of our sakes, start asking God to change you! These next few lessons are mainly about translating "your asking" into tangible concrete steps. Actually, this lesson is something of a teaser because the steps to becoming like Christ require another short book if not our lifetime. The next several lessons lay out the big picture of how God transforms us and considers some first steps. The concluding lessons consider some practical aspects of loving whom God loves – and loving it!

Describe some areas of your life that you wish God to transform:

1. _____

2. _____

3. _____

The Big Picture: Becoming New Creations

Something needs to happen in order for us to behold God himself, even beyond Jesus forgiving our sins! We actually become new creations by . . . dying and rising with Jesus through our Baptism. Consider the following passage:

> You were buried with him in Baptism, in which you were also raised with him through faith in the working of God, who raised him from the dead. And you, who were dead in trespasses and the un-circumcision of your flesh, **God made alive together with him**, having forgiven us all our trespasses, having canceled the bond which stood against us with its legal demands; this he set aside, nailing it to the cross. If then you have been **raised with Christ**, seek the things that are above, where Christ is, seated at the right hand of God. **Put to death** therefore what is earthly in you: fornication, impurity, passion, evil desire, and covetousness, which is idolatry . . . **put on the new nature**, which is being renewed in knowledge after the image of its creator.
>
> Colossians 2:12-14; 3:1,5,10

Didn't know Paul bolded stuff, did you? Put in your own words what Paul says happens to us through Baptism here and in Romans 6.3-11:

_____
_____
_____
_____

How does Paul's "point of view" change in II Corinthians 5:16-17? How would you describe his new perspective?

_____
_____
_____
_____

God's plan for us really defies comprehension. God wants to make us not just any "new creation" or give us just any "new nature" but the very likeness of Jesus himself.

Discussion Questions

1. What's God's biggest challenge in making you a saint? Why?

_____

_____

_____

2. God's grand project of making us "new creations" seems too good to be true. Do you have faith in his plans and ability to carry them out?

_____

_____

_____

Action Items

☐ Prayer/scripture reading of _____ minutes per day

☐ Pray for group member: _____ regarding: _____

☐ Memorize II Corinthians 5.17

Lesson 18 - So Just What are We Going to Look Like?

Yeah, yeah – you got it, right? We're going to look like Jesus sooner or later, at least if we plan on being with God in heaven. What does "being conformed to the image of Jesus" mean exactly? To get started, it may help to consider the "best of the best" human beings you've encountered, then we'll move on to the saints and Jesus himself. Think of some of the people over the course of your life that you loved most or most enjoyed being with, and list them together with what you like most about them:

Favorite People   Prized Traits or Deeds

1. _____
   - _____
   - _____
   - _____

2. _____
   - _____
   - _____
   - _____

3. _____
   - _____
   - _____
   - _____

This exercise helps us begin to imagine what incredible beings God intends to make us. You probably know some pretty wonderful people, which gives us a mere hint of the wonderful creatures God intends to makes us. Yet, unless we happen to be living among fully transformed saints, our holiness and virtue will far surpass the best of what we've seen or experienced of our family, friends, and acquaintances.

The Church does hold up for our imitation and instruction certain men and women overflowing with the power of God's grace, renowned for personal holiness and love of God: canonized saints. Take the docility of Mary, the Mother of God, who through incredible faith accepts the apparent mark of an extramarital affair that often resulted in being stoned to

---

The Ultimate Perfume

Through saints, God spreads in every place the fragrance that comes from knowing him
. . . the aroma of Christ.   II Corinthians 2.14-15

---

death. Considering the lives of those already changed to a large degree into Jesus' likeness gives us a pretty good idea of what we will look like when God's done with us. Read books on the lives of various saints – and imitate them!

Saints are the most beautiful and fascinating of people. Rather than being starchy, prudish and self-satisfied, saints are wonderful and joyful. After all, they have been changed into the image of the One who radiates love, beauty, joy, and goodness. So now you have the answer as to why eternal joy comes from being with God's people as well as with God himself.

What was Jesus really like? What kind of man was he? Fortunately, the gospels paint a pretty good portrait. Describe some of Jesus' qualities depicted in John 11.1-42:

_____
_____
_____
_____

Reasoning again by analogy, consider any virtue and the person who best exemplifies it: comparing their virtue to Jesus' is like comparing a candle to the sun. Indeed, it would be foolish to compare the love, joy, peace, patience, kindness, goodness, faithfulness, gentleness and self control of Jesus with the virtue of any other person. God's love, for starters, is incomparably richer and more tangible than that of any human being. How can God really love me with all my foibles and follies, all my sins and sadness? Look at my history – who could know every moment of my existence and still look upon me with love? With a love so intense that he desires me with him forever, as a friend?

I suggest reading through one of the gospels in one sitting, perhaps Luke (which might take an hour), while asking Jesus to reveal himself more deeply to you. Look particularly for individual encounters Jesus has with various people. You will be amazed at the largeness of God's personality and the richness of his voice speaking to you.

The Best of Men (but then I'm biased)

The morning Dad died I was standing around the kitchen with the priest who was Dad's spiritual director. With a surprising twinkle in his eye, he said, "you know, your father told me it was the best year of his life" (Dad's illness lasted about a year). Just what I had been thinking. And at the funeral Mom said it was hers! Are we a morose lot? Actually, no.

For a guy successful at whatever he put his hand to and full of good friends, a year of struggling with cancer shouldn't be your best. That year did turn Dad from being generally affable and self-contented though sometimes irascible to deeply loving and appreciative, reliable in his tenderness and concern for us. Never, unless you really pried, would he mention the constant discomfort and finally terrible pain from the cancer. In the midst of extreme nausea, for example, he would greet my wife very tenderly and compliment her nice outfit.

Our family saw God transform Dad from a pretty good man into an ideal father and husband, full of fatherly wisdom, holiness and care for others – and funnier than ever. I hope to spend eternity with Dad and people like him.

Application Questions

1. How does God make us better persons?

   _____

   _____

   _____

   _____

   _____

2. What is our role in God making us better persons?

   _____

   _____

   _____

   _____

Action Items

☐ Prayer/scripture reading of _____ minutes per day

☐ Pray for group member: _____ regarding: _____

☐ Read about a saint. If you don't have any books, see http://www.newadvent.org/cathen/index

---

Lesson 19 – Holiness & World View

His divine power has granted to us all things that pertain to life and godliness, through the knowledge of him who called us *to his own glory and excellence,* by which he has granted to us his precious and very great promises, that through these you may escape from the corruption that is in the world because of passion, and *become partakers of the divine nature.*   I Peter 1.3-4

As we have seen, God calls us to be his glorious sons and daughters, to be new creations in Christ that resemble God himself, even, as we see in the above quote, to be partakers in the divine nature! OK, so what does this mean, exactly? God wants to transform all aspects of our lives – our morality and character, our identity, our view of the world, our use of time and resources, those with whom we spend time, and the very pattern of our daily lives[36]. The next couple of lessons consider the following aspects of God's plan for us:

1. to be holy by transforming our morality and character;
2. to see the "world" as he sees it
3. to take our identity as his children; members of his body; temples of the Holy Spirit; stewards; and missionaries.

Lessons 21-24 will consider other practical aspects of how God wishes to transform our lives, while lessons 25-30 then consider God's plan for us to embrace mission

Holiness: Morality & Character

Conversion leads us to life with God and his people. In Baptism, the connection to life with God is instantaneous. If our faith is re-awakened as an adult, repentance and receiving the sacrament of reconciliation immediately re-establishes our life with God and his people. Yet, especially in American society, our lives don't automatically reflect our conversion.

Take a moment and honestly consider the areas of Christian morality with which you struggle (don't worry, you won't be forced to share this if you are working through this book in a small group). In what areas do you struggle most on a daily basis?

_____
_____
_____
_____
_____

Morality and character are interrelated: morality and its embedded values inform us what to do and avoid doing; character is how consistently one lives out a given morality. Osama bin Laden might have terrific character, but screwed up values and morality. Jesus sums up *what to do* as "loving God with all your heart, mind and soul and loving your neighbor as yourself." He also emphatically endorses the Law of Moses for what *not to do*, even making compliance a condition for being with God[37].

After we undergo conversion, our **character** often retains a form based on our former morality or way of living ("living according to the flesh"). All our moral habits make up our character. A habit is moral if it involves doing right or wrong. Possessing honesty is being in the habit of telling the truth. Our moral choices and habits help determine who we are; we slowly become what we choose. Telling lies soon changes you into a liar. One retains the habit of lying even when you want to tell the truth. God needs to transform all of these negative moral habits – vices – into their opposite, as well as create all kinds of good moral habits – virtues – that reflect our new identity as sons and daughters of God, after the pattern of Jesus. The Lord himself discusses character throughout the Sermon on the Mount in Matthew 5-7. Paul discusses the Christian moral life in Romans 12-15; I Corinthians 12-13; Colossians 3-4; Ephesians 4-5, and elsewhere. Paul lists the fruit of the Spirit in Galatians 5[38].

As the Holy Spirit dwells in us, the **fruit of the Spirit** becomes abundant in our lives: love, joy, peace, patience, kindness, goodness, faithfulness, gentleness and self-control[39].

Which fruit of the Spirit do you wish to flourish more in your life?

_____

_____

Do you struggle with whether God's morality is best for you – *its truth*? For example, are you convinced that there is harm in viewing pornography? Or that loving our enemy – even terrorists – is really the right thing to do? Why?

_____

_____

_____

_____

As God is holy, so also must we **become holy**. More than simply "pretty good," God intends for our character to become God-like! God is the source of all goodness; he is pure goodness. Jesus is the measure of perfect righteousness and perfect love. Taking Jesus' character doesn't render dry, rule-following persons striving to do one good deed after another. Rather, God transforms and sets our hearts afire for all that is good, true and beautiful and against all that is evil, false and deformed. All of our passions and appetites come to resemble God's: being and doing "good," even at great personal cost, becomes almost irresistible.

Worldview

*If then you have been raised with Christ, **seek the things that are above**, where Christ is, seated at the right hand of God. Set your minds on things that are above, not on things that are on earth. For you have died, and your life is hid with Christ in God. When Christ who is our life appears, then you also will appear with him in glory.*   Colossians 3.2-4

Creation itself will be set free from its bondage to decay and obtain the glorious liberty of the children of God.   Romans 8.21

Now let's consider the "world" or popular culture. Every worldview is based on a set of values, explicitly or implicitly. Worldly values are expressed in movies, TV, casual conversations, magazines, and internet sites among other places, and include the common ideas on being happy, getting ahead, sex, money, power, relationships, self fulfillment, etc. List and briefly describe some important values of the world:

1. _____

   _____

2. _____

   _____

3. _____

   _____

Although there is some overlap, God's values generally differ from the world's. He primarily sees the potential for tremendous beauty and goodness in every human being and longs for a deep union with each of us. Perhaps God's main work is drawing us into, and making us suitable for, an eternal relationship with him. The *world* is a place for human beings to learn about and exercise their free will in choosing what is good, true and beautiful. Of course, it's also chock full of generally boring but sometimes spectacularly bad choices. Ill-use of ourselves and others (sin) grieves God. Beyond the beauty of creation, God sees little more in the *world* than persons either embracing or rejecting his plan for them to be with him, to become like him and to love what he loves[40]. God sees that those who reject his plan ultimately change into creatures unfit for his company and that of his people. God also sees that some angels who have rejected his plans strive against his plans for us, but that the angels with him (and saints in heaven) join the battle on our behalf.

God put us on earth to know him and to transform us into a creature resembling himself. Our time on earth is a time for growth and transformation. Aside from this eternal perspective, little makes sense. We will die and then God will judge us on whether we have accepted his forgiveness and the grace to become the men and women he wishes us to be – in relationship with him, coming to resemble his goodness, and loving others as he himself does. This grace necessarily issues fruit (Matthew 25); faith without works is a dead faith.

American Catholics no longer – if we ever did – live in a society that reinforces and supports God's plan for our lives. The voracious competition for our values, time, and resources, and how we think about almost every aspect of life is nothing less than a spiritual battle for our very souls. Society in turn feeds and challenges us with materialistic and individualistic values and worldview. How we actually spend our time and discretionary resources usually indicates whether we are living more under the influence of the *world* or according to God's plan for our lives.

Discussion Questions

1. What do you find most troubling about what the world tells us to be? Why?

_____

_____

_____

_____

_____

2. What do you think John Paul II means by a "civilization of love"? How can you contribute?

_____

_____

_____

Action Items

☐ Prayer/scripture reading of _____ minutes per day
☐ Pray for group member: _____ regarding: _____
☐ Memorize Galatians 5.22-23

Lesson 20 - Personal Identity

Sons of God, Members of his Body & Temples of the Holy Spirit

You have received the spirit of sonship. When we cry, "Abba! Father!"
it is the Spirit himself bearing witness with our spirit that we are children of God,
and if children, then heirs, heirs of God and fellow heirs with Christ, provided we suffer with him
in order that we may also be glorified with him.

Romans 8.15-17

How do you think of yourself? What labels or adjectives best describe you, e.g., plumber, student, homemaker, doctor, an American, attractive, funny, Irish, single, son of God, etc.? Just list off what comes to mind without asking how *you should* think of yourself.

1._____

2._____

3._____

4._____

5._____

Our deepest identity should be based on God's unwavering love for us. He knows *you* intimately. He shaped *you* in your mother's womb, knows when *you* sit and when *you* stand, he knows all *your* thoughts, what *you* are going to say before *you* say it; he even has a detailed plan for *your* life (Psalm 139). He loves *you* so incredibly much that he sent his son to make amends for our wrongdoing. He loves us so much that he adopts us as children. Like a good parent, he is completely on our side, he is utterly for us and nothing can separate us from his paternal love (Romans 8.15-39). God's love even has a maternal dimension, comparable to a hen protectively gathering together her chicks (Luke 13.34). Our fundamental identity as God's children is fully secure by God's unwavering love. Describe how you experience your relationship with God the father:

_____
_____
_____
_____

Do you not know that your bodies are members of Christ?
Do you not know that your body is a temple of the Holy Spirit within you,
which you have from God?

I Corinthians 6.15,19

Do we think of ourselves as members of Jesus' body? This identity has both a vertical and horizontal dimension. Vertically, we are organically connected to God, but horizontally to each other. This organic connection is developed throughout I Corinthians and is a major theme of the New Testament. God himself in the person of the Holy Spirit indwells this body. Actually, Scripture refers to indwelling us as individual persons but also indwelling collectively the entire body of Christ, i.e., the Church. The intimacy God intends to have with us is so intense, so dazzling that our language literally fails.

Do we think of ourselves as God does? God sees a person in whom his Spirit dwells, one with whom he is intimately present. God sees us as men and women knit together closely in community, as members of his body, the Church. That is how God sees us.

To become like Jesus we also must think like God, particularly in terms of how we see ourselves. Little does God see and value athletic prowess, intellectual gifts, physical beauty, social attractiveness, or station in life. Rather, in whoever accepts his gift of new life God sees his son or daughter, a member of his household, and one clothed with the dignity of Jesus and filled with his own Spirit.

Missionaries and Stewards

You are not your own;
you were bought with a price.

I Corinthians 6.19

We are ambassadors for Christ,
since God is making his appeal through us.

II Corinthians 5.20

As we take on Jesus' character and holiness and begin to see ourselves as sons and daughters of God, as members of his body, the Church, and as temples of the Holy Spirit, we also take on God's passion for drawing others into a life with himself. Our priorities change! That, or God has more work to do. In fact, we should begin to love one another freely and with joy, even at significant personal cost. And we embrace a missionary life of interceding for, and helping, others to know God.

Our lives are not our own: we are to be about the business of heaven! A mature disciple also recognizes that everything comes from God – all that one has and all that one is. God's power makes us see our very consciousness and human freedom as well as material possessions, education, upbringing (such as it may be), current position, resources, time, health, energy - simply everything - as gifts to further God's plans for our lives and those around us. In short, a mature disciple approaches his life as a steward of God's gifts. What does God expect of us, based on the parable of the talents in Matthew 25.14-30?

_____

_____

_____

Depending on our circumstances, many of us will have time and resources beyond what is required to care for our families to help others: through works of mercy, serving the Church, and evangelism (see the lessons on Mission below). Whatever our circumstances, as God transforms us into the likeness of his Son, caring for those around us and helping people come into a relationship with God becomes our overarching concern.

Take another look at Luke 15, the lesson about what causes Heaven to rejoice. Indeed, the business (and the joy) of heaven is bringing people into heaven! As God's sons or daughters, we take up this Family Business: we take on the identity of missionaries! Throughout his pontificate in too many places to cite, John Paul II strenuously exhorted every Catholic to take up the missionary mandate of Jesus! The U.S. Conference of Catholic Bishops also stresses our identity and duty as missionaries in pastoral documents like _Go and Make Disciples_. We will further consider these themes in the next section on _Mission_.

Discussion Questions

1. How would you like people to remember you when you die?

_____

_____

_____

_____

3. How does the truth that your body is a temple of the Holy Spirit affect your self image?

_____

_____

_____

Action Items

- ☐ Prayer/scripture reading of _____ minutes per day
- ☐ Pray for group member: _____ regarding: _____
- ☐ Share with someone how believers in Christ become sons of God and temples of the Holy Spirit

---

Lesson 21 - Life Choices

> Then Jesus told his disciples, *If any man would come after me, let him deny himself and take up his cross and follow me. For whoever would save his life will lose it, and whoever loses his life for my sake will find it.*
> *For what will it profit a man, if he gains the whole world and forfeits his life?*
> *Or what shall a man give in return for his life?*
>
> Matthew 16.24-26

What does selling everything, laying down our lives and following Jesus actually mean in our daily lives? If following Jesus means following his plan, we must ask our self whether every aspect of our life corresponds to his plan. In the real world, we talk about theory moving into practice as being "where the rubber meets the road." This lesson considers where being a Catholic disciple meets the real world of our choices, time, relationships and resources – which together make up our "pattern of life."

All the decisions related to how we spend our time and resources largely determine our particular **Pattern of Life** or way of life. Our Pattern of Life is comprised of four major components:

- Life Choices
- Daily Routine
- Resources
- Relationships with Family, Friends, and Others

The next several lessons consider the relationship between our Pattern of Life and God's plan for us, beginning with life choices in this lesson.

A Question of Consistency

The overarching question for a disciple is how much our Pattern of Life *supports or expresses* God's plan for our life. What are the **Core Elements of God's plan for our life**? They include:

- A strong prayer and sacramental life
- A Christian personal identity and worldview
- A life of holiness and Christian character
- A life of loving and caring for others
- A strong marriage and family life
- Explicitly Christian fraternal relationships
- A life of mission through intercessory prayer and eagerness to share about Jesus

Real discipleship requires us to soberly assess how our pattern of life reflects and reinforces

God's plan for our life. Failure to tangibly imitate Christ in our daily lives renders us little more than "armchair Christians" – whom the Lord will ultimately disown. What warnings does Matthew 25 provide to this effect?

_____

_____

_____

The scope of this section is limited to asking how our Pattern of Life supports or expresses the core elements of God's plan for our life. How to take on and live out these core elements is one of the goals of the companion to this book, *Made to Be Like Him*.

Life Choices

Let each of you lead the life that the Lord has assigned you, to which God has called you.

I Corinthians 8.17

Life Choices are major directional decisions, such as to one's vocation and career, the location of one's post-secondary schooling, where one lives, choice of a spouse, the type of house in which one lives, how many children to rear, savings and retirement plans, etc. Depending on how old you are, many of these choices may already be made and only some may be changed easily. However, unless we are in the final years of our life, we probably have at least a few major life decisions left relating to work, savings rate and retirement. What major life choices do you face over the next twenty years?

1. _____

2. _____

3. _____

Discussion Question #1. For one of these life choices, describe how your choice may effect the core elements of God's plan for your life (see previous page for listing)?

_____

_____

_____

Discussion Question #2. Why do we need such stiff warnings from the Lord to put "theory into practice"?

_____

_____

Action Items

☐ Prayer/scripture reading of _____ minutes per day

☐ Pray for group member: _____
   regarding a major life choice: _____

Lesson 22 - Daily Routine

Whatever you eat or drink, or whatever you do, do everything for the glory of God.

I Corinthians 10.31

Our daily routine is determined to some degree by our Life Choices and involves work, prayer, leisure, relationships, serving others, etc., but also depends on the priorities we set and our self-discipline. Of course, the demands of school, work, family, and outside commitments can surge from time to time and upset the best laid plans of mice and men! However, our life choices and day to day priorities generally determine our daily routines. For example, how hard we work and how much we play largely determines how much time we have for prayer, caring for our family and others, and maintaining life-giving relationships with other Christians.

The key question is how our daily routine supports and expresses the core elements of God's plan for our lives – and whether we need to change or tweak our routines. Consider how well your daily and weekly activities align with God's plan for you (these questions are meant as primers that hopefully spawn additional questions more applicable to your life).

- ✓ Do we draw out, or linger too much over, our waking up routine?

- ✓ How much do we read the paper each day or surf the web for sports, news, or other interests?

- ✓ How much time do we devote to email?

- ✓ How do we putter away our time?

- ✓ What do we read; what shows or movies do we watch?

- ✓ How often and how long do we stay late at work? Why?

- ✓ How many sports and activities are we (and our kids) involved in?

- ✓ How are we spending Sundays?

- ✓ Do we realistically have time for serving people outside our immediate family?

- ✓ Should we consider spending less time watching or playing sports, of curtailing some other leisure activity, or even downsizing our work or our financial life?

- ✓ How much time do we devote each day to prayer and Scripture reading?

Take an "inventory" of the routine activities that make up your days and weeks and consider how each activity supports or detracts from the core elements of God's plan for your life. Then, put a "+" under any core elements that the activity expresses or reinforces, a "-" under any core elements that the activity undermines.

Daily Activities	Prayer & Sacramental Life	Christian Identity & Worldview	Holiness and Christian Character	Caring for Others	Strong Family Life	Christian Fellowship	Life of Mission
Taking out the trash			+	+			

Weekly Activities

Weekly Activities	Prayer & Sacramental Life	Christian Identity & Worldview	Holiness and Christian Character	Caring for Others	Strong Family Life	Christian Fellowship	Life of Mission
Watching sex-laden TV shows		−	−				

Now consider some additional activities that could express or strengthen the core elements of God's plan for your life:

Core Element	Potential Activity

Core Element   Potential Activity

Strong Prayer &
  Sacramental Life
  • _____
  • _____

Christian Identity &
  Worldview
  • _____
  • _____

Holiness &
  Christian Character
  • _____
  • _____

Caring for others
  • _____
  • _____

Strong family life
  • _____
  • _____

Christian Fellowship
  • _____
  • _____

Life of Mission
  • _____
  • _____

What's Your Experience?

1. Consider a couple of activities that conflict with or undermine a core element of God's plan for your life. Describe how these activities oppose the given core element.

_____

_____

_____

_____

_____

_____

2. Consider a couple of activities that express or strengthen a core element of God's plan for your life. Describe how these activities align with the given core element.

_____

_____

_____

_____

_____

_____

Action Items

- ☐ Prayer/scripture reading of _____ minutes per day
- ☐ Pray for group member: _____ regarding: _____
- ☐ Do at least two of the activities listed on the previous page to strengthen God's plan for your life

Lesson 23 - Resources

Maintain a constant love for one another . . . serve one another with whatever gift each of you has received.
I Peter 4.8-9

As discussed in the last lessons, our particular **Pattern of Life** or way of life is made up of four general areas. The key question for a disciple is how well our Pattern of Life supports God's plan for our life. The reverse is also true: as we embrace God's plan for our life, our Pattern of Life will also change, e.g., growing in our identity as sons and daughters of God will doubtless influence how we relate to others. As we come to understand that the most crucial thing about life is having a relationship with God, our use of time will begin to reflect this central priority. And of course, embracing one aspect of God's plan for our life reinforces other aspects. For example, as we take on a daily prayer life – experiencing the Father's love and grace regularly – we should grow in holiness and our identity as his sons and daughters.

Pattern of Life

- Life Choices
- Daily Routine
- Resources
- Personal Relationships

God's Plan for Our Life

- A strong prayer and sacramental Life
- A Christian self-understanding (or identity) and worldview
- A life of holiness and Christian character
- A life of love and service towards others, starting with one's family
- A strong marriage and family life
- Explicitly Christian fraternal relationships
- A life of mission through intercessory prayer and sharing Jesus with others

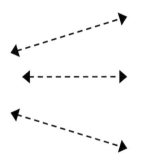

Most people control at least some of the activities that make up our Daily Routine. All of us control with whom we spend leisure time outside the family. When considered objectively, many of us have a substantial amount of discretionary resources. This lesson begins by briefly considering the role of our Resources in God's plan for our life, while the next lesson considers Personal Relationships. This lesson concludes by introducing the question of resources and personal finances[41].

Resources . . . Money, Money, Money

The third measure of our Pattern of Life is resources, the most tangible of which is *moolah*.

Money is more easily measured than the other three elements of our Pattern of Life: Life Choices, Daily Routine, and Personal Relationships. Like the other elements, choices related to money are deeply intertwined with our personal identity, what we value in life, our goals for life, how deliberately we approach life, and, in general, how we embrace God's plan for our lives. In regard to money and resources, this lesson is limited to posing a few general questions.

How does your use of money reflect and support God's plan for your life? Name three instances:

1. _____
2. _____
3. _____

How does your use of money undermine God's plan for your life? Name three specific instances:

1. _____
2. _____
3. _____

> **Which Master?**
>
> No one can serve two masters; for either he will hate the one and love the other, or he will be devoted to the one and despise the other. You cannot serve God and money.   Matthew 6.24

Examination of Budget

Make no mistake: you will be judged by how you use your money. At the end of the day, it is impossible to avoid the connection between discipleship and our use of money. Against any objective measure, even "poor" people living in the West are almost immeasurable better off than even the generation of our grandparents - as measured by disposable income, home size, access to healthcare, education, and life expectancy – and yet we find ourselves often struggling to make ends meet. Could it be that a whole raft of luxuries have become necessities? Consider the following "luxuries" that most of us enjoy in just a couple areas of our lives:

Home Size & Location	$\rightarrow$ More than 1 bedroom per 2 persons
	$\rightarrow$ More than 1 bathroom per 3 persons
	$\rightarrow$ More than 1 eating space and family room
	$\rightarrow$ Attractive neighborhood

Household Expenditures	$\rightarrow$ More than 1 nice dinner at home each week
	$\rightarrow$ Eating out more than once per month
	$\rightarrow$ Desserts at more than 3 meals per week
	$\rightarrow$ Purchase of new clothes each year
	$\rightarrow$ More than 1 car per family
	$\rightarrow$ Driving a car less than 5 years old

Recreational Activities	→ More than 1 week of vacations away per year
	→ More than 1 sport per kid per year
	→ More than 4 tv channels
	→ More than 1 entertainment device per household (tv, ipod, computer, video games, stereo, etc)
	→ Hobbies or sports costing more than 1 week of pay per year

Of course all of these luxuries are wonderful in themselves, but what is their true cost? Both parents working? Working longer hours, in the final analysis, to pay for more such luxuries? Failing to tithe (give 10% to church and charity)? A necessary part of an Examination of Conscience is a periodic scrutiny of our budget. Such an examination of budget considers how *each area* of expenditure supports or detracts from the core aspects of God's plan for our lives, as well as whether our *total household expenditure* supports or detracts from the core aspects of God's plan.

Budgetary Alignment?

1. What are some "essential" items in your budget? What are some "discretionary" items? Discuss the difference between essential and discretionary household spending.

_____

_____

_____

_____

_____

2. Describe the connection between your spending and the simplicity of life discussed in Lesson 1 of Part II.

_____

_____

_____

_____

_____

Action Items

☐ Prayer/scripture reading of _____ minutes per day

☐ Pray for group member: _____ regarding: _____

☐ Review your budget with your wife, a parent, or a close friend.

Lesson 24 - Relationships

Beyond Recreational Friendship

From now on, therefore, we regard no one from a human point of view; even though we once regarded Christ from a human point of view, we regard him thus no longer. Therefore, if any one is in Christ, he is a new creation; the old has passed away, behold, the new has come. II Corinthians 5.16-17

Consider for a moment the big picture: How do you relate to your family and friends? Do you have friends that encourage your relationship with God? Do you have friends that undermine our life with God? Are you helping others regularly? To whom can you turn for help when in need? Do you experience the joy of friendship?

Most of us love to hang out or do stuff with certain people, but many of these relationships have little depth and might be called *Recreational Friendships*. Recreational friendships tend to start and stop while talking over coffee, going to the bar, watching sports, or perhaps at a book club. Recreational friendships usually end when the going gets tough, when you need some help, or simply when the common interest dies. Nothing wrong with recreational friendships, just don't build your life around them or expect them to yield long-term joy. God wants to give us both great joy and encouragement in living for him from deep brotherly and sisterly relationships.

Brothers & Sisters in Christ

As for the saints in the land, they are the noble, in whom is all my delight. Ps 16.3

If we're drawing near to God, we should notice the other people heading in the same direction: they're our brothers and sisters through our common Baptism in Christ. If Baptism makes us sons and daughters of God – we pick up many siblings in the process! On one hand, they are (or will eventually be) a source of great joy. Next to life with himself, God's greatest gifts are relationships with others who are near him. As God makes us like himself we, in turn, are sources of joy to each other. I know it sounds a little too good to be true, but we have a Big God with a Big Plan backed by Big Power and Big Commitment on his part. On the other hand, we love one another, from washing each other's feet to laying down our lives (and everything in between), in direct obedience to the Lord's oft repeated teaching[42]. We help each other with the practical challenges of everyday life, console each other, show kindness - in a word, love our neighbor as ourselves.

I guess on what would be a third hand, God uses us to encourage and help one another live as Christians and to embrace God's entire plan for our life. Many Christians have found joining with others in small groups focused on discipleship – that is, embracing God's plan for our life – to be extremely fruitful. I, for one, doubt I would have continued to embrace God's plan for my life without the encouragement I found in my first couple of small groups.

Loving Others

If you love those who love you, if you do good to those who do good to you, if you lend to those from whom you hope to receive, what credit is that to you? ... Love your enemies, do good, lend, expecting nothing in return. Be merciful as your heavenly father in merciful.
Luke 6.32-36

Aside from our brothers and sisters in Christ and perhaps even more so, God calls us to love those who don't yet know him. While we look and pray for opportunities to help people discover the greatest treasure and joy in life – a relationship with God – we mostly just care for material or emotional needs. Simply esteeming and valuing people from our heart is a profound way of loving others, although caring for our "neighbor" will often be inconvenient and even costly. Of course, as we see in Matthew 25, God expects us to love the particularly needy as if they were Christ himself.

A Question of Alignment

While we love and care first for our spouses and families, to the extent we have time and resources left over, we care for others in tangible ways. More on this in the next lesson. Consider how well our friendships and acquaintances align with God's plan for us (these questions are really meant as primers that hopefully spawn additional questions more applicable to your life).

He's not Goofy, He's my Brother

I thought the guy was a jerk. Well, not a jerk, but at least nerdy. He was tall and lanky. I didn't like his humor. Meet my brother (in Christ) Dave and my new roommate in the fall of 1982. We already got on each other's nerves in the small group we shared, and now we roomed together in a dorm for the sake of evangelism!

To my surprise, by the end of that year we became best friends, closer than blood brothers in a certain way - though still quite different! While Dave moved away, I still consider him a best friend and deeply esteem him. I can't tell you how many men I have grown close to as brothers in Christ since then. I feel like a man grown wealthy with such brotherly friendships.

- ✓ What specific things sustain and strengthen our marriages, such as date nights and regular discussions of family life?
- ✓ What relationships specifically support God's plan for your life?
- ✓ Are you relaxed enough to express kindness in the chance encounters of daily life, even to a retail clerk whose "on-the-job training" is making you late?
- ✓ Are you regularly interceding for God's plan to take root in those around you?

Let's take another "inventory," this time of our friends and acquaintances, and consider how these relationships tend to support or detract from the core aspects of God's plan for us.

Friends

	Prayer & Sacramental Life	Christian Identity & Worldview	Holiness and Christian Character	Caring for Others	Strong Family Life	Christian Fellowship	Life of Mission
Cousin Rick			+		+	+	

Acquaintances

	Prayer & Sacramental Life	Christian Identity & Worldview	Holiness and Christian Character	Caring for Others	Strong Family Life	Christian Fellowship	Life of Mission
Co-worker		−	−				

What's Your Experience?

1. Consider a relationship that *conflicts with or undermines* a core element of God's plan for your life. Describe how the relationship opposes the given core element.

   _____

   _____

   _____

2. Consider a relationship that *expresses or strengthens* a core element of God's plan for your life. Describe how the relationship aligns with the given core element.

   _____

   _____

   _____

Action Items

☐ Prayer/scripture reading of _____ minutes per day

☐ Pray for group member: _____ regarding: _____

☐ Get together with one of the members of your men's group

Summing it All Up

As we have seen in this section, God wants to transform nearly every aspect our lives in very concrete ways. Rather than a figure of speech, God literally wants to make us new creations after the pattern of his own son, Jesus. For you diagram buffs, the following is one way to picture the various aspects of transformation.

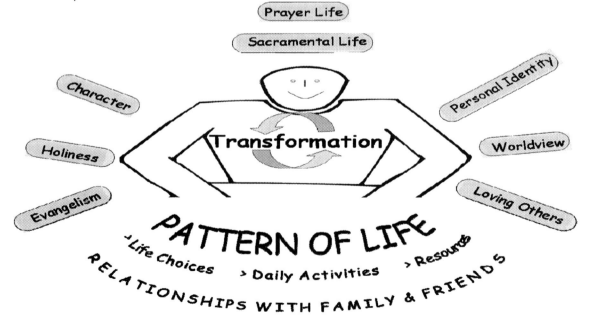

——— Embracing Mission ———
(Loving Whom God Loves)

"As the Father has sent me, so I send you"

Lesson 25 – The Call to Love Others

The Mother Teresa Syndrome

Being a liberal arts major, I soon realized what a duck-out-of-water I was in business school. Desiring a family and without the prospect of gainful employment, I found myself in a school I hated – yet I stayed. Though already a practicing Catholic, I was hardly immune to the allure of fame, fortune and power in the world of business. But where was the joy in my classmates? Some found joy in creative course work. God certainly gives pleasure in exercising his gifts – which is true in any kind of work we do, however aesthetic and creative (most business schoolwork involves little of either). While my classmates had lots of drive and passion, I saw little joy. Against this backdrop, I experienced something of an epiphany while traveling to Asia after graduation.

I spent a good deal of the eighteen-hour plane ride to Singapore reading about a figure soaring in popularity at the time: Mother Teresa. The contrast between Mother Teresa and her gang of nuns and my business school buddies couldn't have been greater. A larger culture clash is hard to imagine. Talk about hero worship - go hang out in a top business school for a few days, where everybody wants to be a *gazillionaire*. Everybody wants to run a major corporation. You spend much of the two years picturing yourself in different roles of power, imagining people looking up to you, and thinking about what wonderful and creative things you'll soon be doing . . . how much you'll be loved (or envied) for your accomplishments and position - all this to speak nothing of the gratifications of making and spending tons of money. There was little confusion in business school about what makes you happy: a job with fat pay and a promising career track. Did I mention making money, lots of money?

Now cut to me alone for an eighteen-hour flight, quite isolated from the business school culture, reading story after story about this diminutive lady spending four hours a day on her knees in prayer, ten hours caring for the worst of the worst, then refreshing herself in the squalor of her dingy quarters over a bowl of watery soup . . . followed by more prayer and a short night on straw. A pretty riveting and ecstatic existence, wouldn't you say?

I didn't think so. Certainly not the American recipe for joy and happiness. Yet a certain joy sparkles – even flashes– from her face, filling the room. Young women, from good homes and bad, swell her ranks of do-gooders. Many see in her the face of joy and the face of Christ. Many great people of the world sought her out; some came to faith in Christ through her witness. I had rarely met such joy as Mother Teresa's and the Sisters of Charity. If anyone was happy on earth, paradoxically, it was these women! A more perfect opposite of the typical business school grad is hard to find (not that we are really such a bad lot).

Like Father, Like Son: Joy in Loving Others

> *I delight to do your will, O my God; your law is within my heart.*
>
> Psalm 40.8

How do you account for the culture-defying joy of Mother Teresa? It's in the genes, you might say. Mother Teresa's genes, however, aren't unique; in fact, I'm actually talking about some pretty amazing genes common to us all. Read Genesis 1.26-27 and describe what it says about our "genetic" makeup:

_____

_____

_____

_____

You didn't really need to read this excerpt from the Creation story to get the point. We already know from our study in the last lesson that God makes us a new creation after the pattern of

Jesus. Does God making us like Jesus change our motivations and life goals? As we more and more reflect the image of Christ, do we also begin doing what Jesus does? One can only chuckle at the force of this logic.

→ **Why ?????**

→ **How ?????**

→ **Won't it be boring ?????**

On a certain level, the proper response to God's plan for us to not only *become like Jesus* but to *do what Jesus does* is sheer terror. In fact, God wishes so thoroughly to transform our hearts that we come *to love* whom he loves. We will take up these questions of why, how, and boredom in the next lesson.

God's love has been poured into our hearts through the Holy Spirit which has been given to us.

Romans 5.5

What's Your Experience?

1. Consider Mother Teresa or someone you admire who radically serves others. What impresses you about them?

   _____
   _____
   _____

2. Why does helping others make us happy?

   _____
   _____
   _____

Action Items

☐ Prayer/scripture reading of _____ minutes per day
☐ Pray for group member: _____ regarding: _____
☐ Memorize Romans 5.5

Lesson 26 – What We Were Made For

God created man in his image, in the image of God he created him.

Genesis 1.27

Why? – You Can't Help It!

Since God made us in his image – lost in the Garden of Eden through sin but restored by being born anew in Christ – as we conform more and more to this image, we can't help but love whom God loves. God has designed or programmed us for loving others as he does. What are God's basic motivations and goals? How do John 3.16-17 and I John 4.7-12 describe these?

_____

_____

_____

_____

Of course, on our bad days we can sometimes, shall we say, *override the program*. Until God transforms away our "bad days": even if we don't "feel like it" we love others in obedience to Jesus' command. What does Jesus command in John 15.12-13?

_____

_____

_____

How? – By God's Power

The *Catechism* puts it this way, picking up one of the main themes of John 15:

> The Savior himself comes to love, in us, his Father and his brethren, our Father and our brethren. His person becomes, through the Spirit, the living and interior rule of our activity. (CCC 2074)

Indeed, loving others is a God-thing – meaning that God not only has to point the way but also supply the power. Read John 15 verses 1-5 and 12-13. Yes, there it is again. Repetition may madden, but I bet you've got this passage down by now. What is the key to loving others according to these passages? How do we accomplish this?

_____

_____

You may wish to review the section on *Equipping for Battle*.

Boring . . . or Source of Great Joy?

God delights in the human beings he has created – see Genesis 1.26-7. God also delights in bringing people to himself – take a look at the great joy of the father welcoming home his once evil son in the story of the Prodigal Son (Luke 15).

Wonder what motivates God? Isn't "love" *something you do*? Actually, I think it's ultimately more like *something you are* (or become). Now, why would anyone wish to become like Mother Teresa? I think the simple reason is that it ultimately gives us joy. Of course, if the person we love doesn't require the supreme sacrifice like Jesus' death on the Cross– so much the better. If we really love someone, we cherish their good above our own and it gives us joy.

Look at the strange paternal love that drives parents to make sacrifices for the sake of bettering their children or to rescue their baby from a burning house. Ultimately, we can't know *why* loving us gives God pleasure or why loving others so fills the Sisters of Charity with joy. All we can say is – *it does*! It's just how God is, and

> **What's Dr. Seuss got to do with it?**
>
> Sam cajoles his reluctant buddy into trying green eggs and ham: "Try them! Try them! And you may. Try them and you may, I say."
>
> *Just give loving others a try.*
>
> Your response may parallel that of Sam's buddy: "I do so like green eggs and ham! Thank you! Thank you, Sam-I-am."

consequently, how we ourselves are programmed. Being made in the image of God, "the practice of goodness is accompanied by spontaneous spiritual joy and moral beauty"[43]. This joy or pleasure comes from the work of Christ in us through the Holy Spirit:

> Moral perfection consists in man's being moved to the good not by his will alone, but also by his sensitive appetite, as in the words of the psalm: "My heart and flesh sing for joy to the living God." (CCC 1770) [The] law of love makes us act out of the love infused by the Holy Spirit. (1972)

The "spontaneity" with which spiritual joy and moral beauty will accompany our practice of goodness will vary with each individual, based on factors such as personality, legacy sin, etc. In other words, it may take a bit of time before we rejoice over doing the dishes or changing diapers!

What's Your Experience?

1. Describe an experience of joy, satisfaction or pleasure in helping other people.

_____

_____

2. Would you expect to have more joy over scrimping and saving in order to help feed a hungry person or to buy an expensive car for your child? Why?

_____

_____

_____

_____

Action Items

- ☐ Prayer/scripture reading of _____ minutes per day
- ☐ Pray for group member: _____ regarding: _____
- ☐ Help someone who has no reason to expect your help

Lesson 27 – Our Mission: Family & Intercessory Prayer

Love your neighbor as yourself   Luke 10.27

You too go into the vineyard   Matthew 20.7

As God transforms our lives to resemble that of Jesus' in terms of who we are, how we think, what we feel, and how we relate to the Father and other human beings, we also come to love whom God loves. The godly sense of loving something is to ascribe to it infinite value and relate to it accordingly. Loving gold implies hoarding gold. Loving others implies caring for others and advancing their interests. Let's consider some of the ways God would have us do this. Jesus' love has two practical dimensions: caring for people's needs and bringing people into a relationship with God.

What each of us is able to, and must, do is care for our families, pray for the coming of the kingdom and simply love everyone around us – friends, co-workers, fellow students, acquaintances, the fast-food clerk, strangers we come across – by small (and sometimes large)

acts of kindness. Also, we must be prepared to share our faith with anyone with whom we come across in our daily lives. Taken together, these mandates comprise our **Primary Mission**. Many are called to a **Secondary Mission** of more active evangelism – joining the Church in her global mobilization to the *New Evangelization*, serving in the parish, or performing works of mercy. After briefly considering our primary missions of caring for our families and intercession, the next lesson challenges us to deploy some of our remaining discretionary time to take on a secondary mission outside the home. This section on Mission concludes with two lessons on evangelism.

Families First

Therefore a man leaves his father and his mother and cleaves to his wife,
and they become one flesh.　　　　　　　　　Genesis 2.24

God first calls us to love those who are in our immediate midst as he loves them. We are to *love our spouses* as Christ loves the Church. We are to *love one another* as Jesus loves us, again, from washing one another's feet to laying down our lives. We are to *care for our children* just as God would. Therefore, we first express our love for those who are already in our midst, foremost those whom God has already entrusted to us, our immediate families.

What are some practical ways you have loved and cared for your parents, spouse or children in the last week?

❖ _____

❖ _____

❖ _____

Intercession: Thy Kingdom Come

Read Matthew 6.8-15. Ponder the meaning of the first petition Jesus asks us to pray (verse 10). What do you suppose this means?

_____

_____

_____

_____

_____

Praying for God's kingdom to come probably points to several things but there can be little doubt the primary meaning is *for others to enter the kingdom of God* – *"May your kingdom come"* (into the lives of all human beings). Far from being the exclusive role of monks, God calls us all to enter a nonstop life of praying for other people to embrace God's plan for their lives. Interceding for others is the stuff of daily commutes, trips to the grocery store, even while showering. A life of intercession supplements rather than replaces a more concentrated daily time of prayer. While we might begin the day with Mass, Scripture reading or a personal prayer time, we fill odd bits of time throughout the day with intercession. Such a life of daily intercession is no less important to bringing others into the riches of life with God than the preaching of a great evangelist. A life of daily intercession should characterize the homebound person no less or more than the career evangelist or your parish priest. Intercession is a tangible and crucial way all of the people of God are called to join in the saving priestly work of Jesus.

Discussion Questions

1. How can we safeguard against serving outside the home undermining our family life?

   _____
   _____
   _____

2. Why does Scripture place so much emphasis on interceding for others?

   _____
   _____
   _____

Action Items

- ☐ Prayer/scripture reading of _____ minutes per day
- ☐ Pray for group member: _____ regarding: _____
- ☐ Pray through your intercessory list from Lesson 7

Lesson 28 – Our Mission: Serving in the Field

Share in suffering for the gospel   II Timothy 1.8

God expects us to align soberly our Pattern of Life with his priorities, as discussed in Lessons 21-24. After aligning our lives with God's plan, many will find time for serving God's kingdom outside of our homes, at least during some periods of our lives. Of course, we care for whomever happens to cross our paths (Luke 10.30-37). While we have to be wise about not giving away time and money we don't have, the Lord wants us to care for the neighbor in need who chances across our path. Many of us will be able to get involved outside our homes in ways beyond the chance need or crisis of a "neighbor." Read Matthew 25:31-46 and list the specific ways that God will judge what we do with the incredible resources he lavishes upon our society[44]:

❖ _____

❖ _____

❖ _____

❖ _____

The opportunities for those able to serve outside their homes on a regular basis may be grouped into the following categories. List some specific ways you might serve for each category, e.g., becoming involved in the Knights of Columbus as a Work of Mercy (raises money for charity):

- Evangelism (perhaps the most pressing area)

    1) _____

    2) _____

    3) _____

- Supporting the internal life of the parish and the Church

    1) _____

    2) _____

    3) _____

- Works of Mercy, whether sponsored by your parish or otherwise

    1) _____

2) _____

3) _____

Application Questions

1. Take some time to consider soberly and prayerfully your ability to serve outside your home. What daily, weekly or monthly activities, if any, might you replace with time spent serving others outside the home?

   _____
   _____
   _____

2. Which category and specific services most interest you? Do you feel God calling you to something in particular? Why?

   _____
   _____
   _____
   _____

Action Items

☐ Prayer/scripture reading of _____ minutes per day
☐ Pray for group member: _____ regarding: _____
☐ Ask someone who knows you well to recommend an area of service for you

---

Lesson 29 – Our Mission: Evangelism

The most valuable gift that the Church can offer to the bewildered and restless world of our time is to form within it Christians who are confirmed in what is essential and who are humbly joyful in their faith.[45]

We are like the person who found the treasure and sold everything to possess it (Matthew 13.44). The treasure is our relationship with God and his people, a treasure so rich and overflowing that giving it away can't diminish it. God wants our hearts to burn for others to possess the surpassing riches of knowing God. All disciples of Jesus should be ready to share their faith[46]. Read Matthew 28.18-20 to see what Jesus says more specifically – what exactly does Jesus command? How can you respond to this command?

_____
_____
_____
_____
_____
_____

As we can see, Jesus concludes his earthly ministry by sending his disciples forth to bring all nations into a relationship with him. The overall theme of John Paul II's pontificate may be the *New Evangelism*, the call to bring people into a relationship with God through Jesus, particularly those who are nominally or culturally Christian. Well, easier said than done, as the adage goes ... except that Jesus never asked anyone to share his good news without some help. Read Acts 1.4-8. What kind of big-time help does Jesus offer?

_____
_____

This help is available to us as well[47]. How to tap into it? Just like in becoming like Jesus, in order to share about Jesus we have to ask for God's power. We ask for love and confidence in our sharing. Above all, we ask God to draw specific people to himself and then look for opportunities to share gently our "good news" about Jesus (the gospel) with them.

List five people to begin praying for right now (and continue to do so at least weekly):

❖ _____

❖ _____

❖ _____

❖ _____

❖ _____

How about the basics of sharing the gospel with others? You don't have to be perfect nor have everything all figured out. The only requirement is embracing and treasuring your life with God. The main point is, God calls all of us to be ready to share, not just priests or professional evangelists. In fact, better to avoid fancy theological language, whoever you are. Best simply to share about how you came into, or became more deeply aware of, your relationship with God and to share some way in which God has changed you. Of course, *some* preparation is helpful and we will work on sharing the good news in the next lesson.

Application Questions

1. Describe your own (adult) conversion, i.e., when you became serious about your faith. Break your experience down into three or four steps including how your life was changed. Practice sharing your story in your group; shorten your story to under 5 minutes.

   _____

   _____

   _____

   _____

   _____

   _____

   _____

   _____

   _____

   _____

   _____

   _____

2. Should your group be open to adding new people? Why or why not?

   _____

   _____

   _____

   If so, should a few guys begin a group to take the new guys through this book?

   _____

   _____

   _____

Action Items

☐ Prayer/scripture reading of _____ minutes per day
☐ Pray for group member: _____ regarding: _____
☐ Identify 3 men to invite to a new small group and begin praying for them

---

Lesson 30 – How to Share Our Faith

In Our Own Words

In this lesson you will do less reading and more writing! Consider again the opening paragraph of the US Bishops' discussion of qualities of mature adult faith and discipleship:

> At the heart of all we are and do as the Church is a revelation of great Good News: God, who is love, has made us to enjoy divine life in abundance, to share in the very life of God, a communion with the Holy Trinity together with all the saints in the new creation of God's reign. Faith, which is a gift from God, is our human response to this divine calling: It is a personal adherence to God and assent to his truth. Through searching and growth, conversion of mind and heart, repentance and reform of life, we are led by God to turn from the blindness of sin and to accept God's saving grace, liberating truth, and sustaining love for our lives and for all of creation.[48]

Before reading ahead, give some thought to how you would explain conversion to a non-believer or to a confused and hardly practicing or non-practicing Catholic. Read the CCC 1987-97 for a short description of these truths[49] and review the discussion of conversion in Part I, Lessons 2 and 5.

Application Question #1. Describe the most central truths of the gospel.

A. _____

B. _____

C. _____

D. _____

E. _____

F. _____
_____
_____
_____

Application Question #2. What steps are necessary to embrace life with God?

A. _____

_____

B. _____

_____

C. _____

_____

D. _____

_____

Application Question #3. What is the basis for a disciples' joy?

_____

_____

_____

_____

Exercise

1. Practice giving 3-5 minutes explanations of the basic gospel truths, in your own words, as listed in the above Application Exercises. Each member should have at least two chances to do this – learn from each other!

2. What are some ways to steer a casual conversation, over breakfast, say, into an opportunity to share about your conversion?

_____

_____

_____

_____

Action Items

☐ Prayer/scripture reading of _____ minutes per day

☐ Pray for group member: _____ regarding: _____

☐ Meet with each of the three guys you have been praying for and invite them to attend the celebration your group is having to mark the end of its Discipleship Phase (see next lesson's format)

Lesson 31 - Celebration

I hope that God has worked powerfully in your lives. "Basic construction" of your life as a disciple should be well underway, if not complete, including the following elements:

- A strong prayer and sacramental life
- A Christian personal identity and worldview
- A life of holiness and Christian character
- A life of love and caring for others
- A strong marriage and family life
- Explicitly Christian fraternal relationships
- A life of mission through intercessory prayer and an eagerness to share about Jesus to others

Our foundation is conversion, while a solid prayer and sacramental life fuels our ongoing transformation and life of charity and mission. For our part, we have put the Lord on the throne of our lives, yielding ourselves without reservation. We have aligned our Pattern of Life with God's plan in terms of our life choices, daily routine, relationships with others, and personal finances.

This lesson is simply having a celebration.

> **Not So Humble Thanksgiving!**
>
> Oh God, thank you for making me so perfect. so loving, so kind, a model for my men's group, a light to those in darkness . . .

A Celebrative Toast

Now that you see with spiritual eyes you probably realize that God has all sorts of plans for further "improvements and additions" to your life. Perfecting the life of holiness, prayer, serving others, getting our life in perfect order, etc., will take a bit longer than the months that you've invested in this book. Perhaps you have had to confront some very deep hurts or personal weaknesses due to earlier patterns of sin that will need some significant help.

Your life of discipleship is probably going very well thus far – rejoice and be glad. Some of you, however, may be somewhat frustrated by the slowness of progress or from legacy sin (see the end of Lesson 13), be of good cheer. You have made substantial progress and you have a heavenly Father who has counted every hair of your head – you are extremely precious to him, whatever your shortcomings or problems. God is deeply committed to fully transforming your life, however difficult and long that may take, with great love and gentleness.

If you have been working through this book with some other disciples, make this meeting celebrative. You may wish to have a nice dinner together or simply bring some particularly festive drinks and desserts. Let your time of prayer together be primarily thanksgiving for all that God has done for you. Honor what God has done in each of your lives.

Take some time to consider three areas of your life that God has transformed.

➢ _____

➢ _____

➢ _____

Consider how God has worked in each member of your group. List growth in a particular virtue, holiness, changes in how they live, how they have been encouraging, etc.

Group Member	Area of Growth or Transformation
_____	_____
_____	_____
_____	_____
_____	_____
_____	_____
_____	_____

I suggest thanking God for the ways he has worked in your life during your group's time of thanksgiving prayer. Of course, do so in a spirit of humility! Then, during your meal or dessert and drinks, let each member first share how God has worked in your life through your men's group. Then, honor each other for ways in which God has been at work. Make such honoring of each other a tradition on your birthdays.

Action Items

☐ Prayer/scripture reading of _____ minutes per day
☐ Pray for group member: _____ regarding: _____
☐ Pray about how God can use your group or members of your group to evangelize and disciple others

---

Lesson 32 - The Road Ahead

So where do we go from here? Do you wish to continue meeting as a group? Review Lesson 6 of Part I. What purposes listed in "Specifics of Making Jesus Lord of Our Men's Group" does your men's group fulfill?

_____

_____

_____

_____

Reading the Map

Do you feel that the group has successfully completed Phase II described in the section "Life Cycle of a Men's Group pursuing Discipleship"? Why or why not?

_____

_____

_____

_____

What are some specific ways your men's group can move into Phase III, "Kingdom Living"?

_____

_____

_____

_____

While your group may wish to take a short break from "discipleship stuff," consider what areas of discipleship are you most interested in working on next. Which topics on the "Discipleship Map" on the following page are you interested in further pursuing?

➢ _____

➢ _____

➢ _____

Some criteria for selecting an area for your group to pursue next include:

- what is most helpful for each of the guys;
- what materials are available that are appropriate for this group; and
- what guys are most interested in studying.

Discipleship Map
A Listing of Transformation and Mobilization for Mission Topics

Aspects of Transformation

- Develop a strong prayer and sacramental life
    - Develop a life of prayer and Scripture study
    - Understand the Mass and other sacraments
- Form a Christian Personal Identity and Worldview
    - Core Aspects of a Believer's Identity
    - Elements of a Christian Worldview
- Grow in Holiness and the Character of Christ
    - Basics: Sin, Conscience, Grace and Holiness
    - Character Transformation: freedom from serious sin, practice of Christian virtues, and growth in the fruit of the spirit and emotional maturity
- Develop a Christian Pattern of Life
    - Elements: Life Choices, Daily Routine, Relationships and Resources
    - Align one's Pattern of Life to support the Core Elements
        - A strong prayer and sacramental life
        - A Christian personal identity and worldview
        - A life of holiness and Christian character
        - A life of love and caring for others
        - A strong marriage and family life
        - Explicitly Christian fraternal relationships
        - A life of mission
- Live as Stewards of God's Gifts
- Develop strong Fraternal Christian Friendships
- Develop a strong Marriage and Family Life

Mission

- Love your "neighbors" by cheerfully helping them
- Receive general training on Intercession and Evangelism
- Identify and embrace a mission (for those able to serve beyond caring for their family): evangelism, supporting internal parish life, or works of mercy

Finishing the Journey

What to study? Review the following Roadmap for Selected Men's Group Resources. You may also wish to consult NFCM.org and GodsPlanforYourLife.org websites, and other sources[a]. In light

---

[a] For a comprehensive list of resources dealing with pornography and sexual purity, please see www.dads.org/struggleswithporn.asp.

of your interests above, which books or resources most appeal to you?

➤ _____

➤ _____

➤ _____

The facilitator will lead the group in coming to a conclusion about the next book or resource to consider together.

A ROADMAP FOR SELECTED MEN'S GROUP RESOURCES

The Catholic men's group resources on the NFCM website are broken down into five categories: Living as a Catholic Man, Marriage and Family, Spiritual Life, John Paul II, Eucharist, and Evangelization. The National Fellowship of Catholic Men is committed to providing high quality resources for use in men's fellowship groups, or for individual study, including over 12 new ones in the past year and a half. In addition to the books that can be purchased directly from the NFCM, an additional 25 on a variety of topics of interest to Catholic men are also available on the NFCM website. These books can be ordered through direct links to various online web bookstores. Below is a roadmap for a few selected resources from the first three categories.

Living As A Catholic Man

Signposts, How to be a Catholic Man in the World Today by Bill Bawden and Tim Sullivan. *Signposts* was specifically developed by two Catholic deacons who are heavily involved in the Catholic men's movement, and is ideal for a small-group setting or individual study. This is by far the most popular of our men's resources. This powerful resource uses Scripture and Catechism references, short real life stories, and challenging questions to aid in the group discussion. The individual lessons are broken down into four different categories: Man and God, The Measure of a Man, Man and Family, and Man and His World.

Brothers! Calling Catholic Men into Vital Relationship by Geoff Gorsuch helps build strong relationships with other Catholic men as brothers in Christ, This Catholic version of a popular men's movement book uses the baseball diamond to represent the process of building vital relationships with other Catholic men: first base is where we learn to "accept one another," second base where we develop our friendships, third base where we "exhort one another" in facing life's challenges together, and home plate is where we grow in Christlikeness. Each chapter ends with excellent discussion questions for the men's group.

Boys to Men, The Transforming Power of Virtue, by Tim Gray and Curtis Martin, helps men live virtuous lives. Each chapter is on a different virtue, with challenging questions, using Scripture passages, at the end of each chapter.

If your group wants to grow deeper spiritually, consider using *Spiritual Workout of a Former Saint* by Danny Abramowicz, former All-Pro wide receiver for the New Orleans Saints. This is an excellent resource for Catholic men's groups. It is more than the story of a recovering alcoholic grabbing onto - and working hard at - his second chance at a happy, spiritually rich life. This book, based on proven NFL workout techniques, is a practical, encouraging, step-by-step method to help you grow spiritually; add new life to your relationships with the your spouse, family, and friends; and re-energize your soul as you deepen your love of Christ and His Church.

Marriage And Family

If your group wants to go deeper in understanding solid principles on how fathers and grandfathers can have a positive effect on their children's (and grandchildren's) lives, consider using *Velvet and Steel, A Practical Guide for Christian Fathers and Grandfathers* by John Ream. This book also provides practical ways for husbands to be more effective fathers and to relate to their wives as full partners in marriage and family life. It has excellent discussion questions at the end of each chapter.

For fathering, marriage, and family, two 3-cassette tape series are available: *Restoring the Hearts of Fathers* by Curtis Martin and *Safeguarding the Family* by Philip Gray, Curtis Martin, and Marcus Grodi. In a day when so many men fail to meet the challenges and responsibilities of marriage and family life, Curtis Martin speaks a clear word in *Restoring the Hearts of Fathers*, At the same time lighthearted and heavy hitting, Martin calls modern men to be true men, husbands and fathers. Three of today's most insightful Catholic apologists light the way for families in the modern age in the *Safeguarding the Family* series, including "Marriage, the Forgotten Sacrament" by Philip Gray, "Becoming Men of God" by Curtis Martin, and "Keeping Our Kids Catholic", by Marcus Grodi.

Spiritual Life

Embracing the Kingdom: A Bible Study on Conversion by Rich Cleveland, is a Bible study on important aspects of our spiritual life. This study emphasizes applying God's Word in Scripture to our daily lives, and consists of 11 lessons on the importance of Scripture, prayer, community, conversion, and faith.

Mission of the Messiah by Tim Gray, is a bible study on the Gospel of Luke. This study presents the messianic mission of Jesus as the fulfillment of Old Testament prophecy. It also shows how the plan of God revealed in the Old Testament is fulfilled in the life, death, and resurrection of Jesus Christ. The review questions at the end of each chapter provide fresh material for group discussion (or individual reflection).

Mystery of the Kingdom by Edward P. Sri, is a bible study on the Gospel of Matthew. This study focuses on the "kingdom of God" and why it is the heart of Jesus' teaching. The provocative study questions at the end of each chapter make this book ideal for group study (or individual study).

Suggestions for Group Study

The following is a summary of suggestions for Group Study that are elaborated in Part I, Lesson 6 and in the Appendix on Group Discipleship Dynamics.

1. Agree on a discussion group leader (facilitator). The facilitator helps people who talk too little talk more and those who talk a lot, well, talk less! The facilitator also helps maintain the group's focus on the given lesson, avoid bogging down on peripheral issues, and maintain a positive atmosphere. In fact, these are the responsibilities common to whole group. The facilitator is not (normally) a theological or biblical expert. The facilitator paces the discussion of the interpretation and application questions in each lesson. See www.GodsPlanforYourLife.org or www.ParishLifeServices.org to download facilitator guides for each lesson.

2. Open with Prayer. The prayer may be the *Lord's Prayer*, one or more worshipful songs, or any other type of prayer. The emphasis should be on inviting God to enliven the discussion with the Holy Spirit – after all, the whole point is to encounter the living God and allow him to transform and inspire you!

3. Spend at least ½ hour preparing each lesson. Of course, sometimes life does get hectic and we don't prepare as much as we hope. Normally, there is time to further ponder the interpretation and discussion questions when the group meets. Also, selections of each lesson may be read during the meeting.

4. Discuss the material in a positive way. Smile and be attentive to each other. Encourage each other to know the Lord more deeply and embrace his plan for our life! Be sure to provide time for each person to speak.

5. Keep the Focus on Jesus and the Holy Spirit. The focus is on practically applying God's word in your life, not deep theological enquiry. Focus on how to appropriate God's grace in your life rather than subtle theological questions. When challenging questions come up, appoint someone from the group to ask your pastor or the overall men's ministry leader, or to consult the *Catechism of the Catholic Church*.

6. Maintain Candor and Confidentiality. Discussing your relationship with God involves our personal life and feelings, as does discussing how to more fully embrace God's plan for our lives.

7. Pray for one another. Close each meeting with each person offering a prayer request, for which the group then prays silently for fifteen seconds. Close with either the *Lord's Prayer* or a *Hail Mary*. Pray for each others' requests at least one time during the week.

8. Start and finish promptly. People may linger afterwards or all agree to continue the discussion, but people should always be free to leave at the agreed upon time.

About the Author & Acknowledgements

Peter Ziolkowski is the director of Parish Life Services ("PLS"), a non-profit organization devoted to promoting the New Evangelization and practical faith formation in Catholic parishes. PLS also publishes two websites related to evangelization, practical faith formation and parish renewal: www.GodsPlanforYourLife.org and www.ParishLifeServices.org. In addition to working with parishes and groups, all associates of PLS are committed to personally sharing the gospel with those in their midst and helping others grow as disciples. Peter is also a member of Emmaus Journey, a Catholic organization dedicated to evangelism and discipleship.

Mr. Ziolkowski has been active in evangelism and adult faith formation since 1987 in diverse areas ranging from collegiate ministry, directing adult faith formation and hosting a Catholic radio show. Peter currently directs evangelism and small groups at Christ the King parish and has taught a course on Scripture at Sacred Heart Major Seminary in Detroit. Peter lives in Ann Arbor, Michigan with his wife, Theresa, and their five children.

Mr. Ziolkowski would like to acknowledge the careful reading and numerous suggestions of his colleague at Parish Life Services, Elizabeth Siegel, and Fr. Bill Baer and Dr. Dan Keating, who were my first adult spiritual mentors. Of course, I write out the context of my own community of faith centered, to some degree, on Christ the King parish, but extending to include many others. Finally, the comments of my wife Theresa have improved this book substantially; she has been a ongoing encouragement.

Appendix: Group Discipleship Dynamics

This Appendix covers some of the group discipleship dynamics that are helpful for a group in a discipleship phase, discussed in Part I, Lesson 6. Such discipleship dynamics include:

Area	Group Dynamic
Basics Skills	Attendance, prep and enthusiasm
	Maintain group focus
	Balanced participation by all group members
Team Captain	Servant Leadership
	Facilitator Duties
Game Plan	Focus on personal application, not theological enquiry
	Pose universal questions; Seek individual answers
	Recognize that "one size doesn't fit all" in terms of personal prayer time, use of our time, individual gifting, etc.
Teamwork	Zeal for pursuing God's plan for our lives
	Strive together as peers
	Love and pray for one another
Making Plays	Make group a "safe place" to share about our goals, challenges, failures, and successes
	Role of goal setting and accountability
	Safeguard personal autonomy in decision making
	Tackling deep-seated problems & finishing strong

This Appendix assumes familiarity with, and builds upon, the sections on "meeting format" and "general operating principles" from "A Starter Kit for Catholic Men's Groups", and the sections on the "role of a facilitator" and the "value of small group discussions" from "A Starter Kit for Catholic Men's Group Facilitators[50]".

TEAM CAPTAIN

Servant Leadership

It is worth emphasizing that a facilitator's role is one of service to the group. When there is work to do, either someone volunteers or is designated to do it or it doesn't get done! And facilitating is indeed work. If you happen to be in a group with a lot of "natural leaders", each man should be quite appreciative of the one who puts in the work to facilitate the group effectively. Any kind of leadership in the body of Christ must be informed by the Lord's example. Read Mark 10:45. In what ways does Jesus demonstrate servant leadership?

Facilitator Duties

The duties articulated in the "Starter Kit for Catholic Men's Group Facilitators" include:

- helping set meeting times and places
- leading by example in attendance, preparation, and enthusiasm
- maintaining the group's focus on the meeting's topic
- ensuring that all members have an opportunity to participate

"Gee Guys, seems like a lot of protective gear for such a small chlorine gas leak"

In the discipleship phase, the facilitator also takes responsibility for, and encourages, the team to stick to the game plan, work as a team, and simply make plays, as discussed in this Appendix. Somebody is probably already facilitating your group, at least informally. Is the existing facilitator willing to invest more in the group during the discipleship phase? Are others interested in facilitating? If so, are they prepared to invest some time in study and training to improve their facilitating skills? If more than one person is interested in facilitating, the group may follow these guidelines:

1) Rotate facilitators every six months, at least during the discipleship phase.
2) If the incumbent facilitator wishes to continue, he serves for the first six months.
3) If there is no existing facilitator, let the group discuss their preferences over who takes the first term. If discussion fails to clarify who should take the first term, flip a coin.
4) Whether or not leadership is being rotated, at the end of every six months, spend a session as a group evaluating group dynamics. Only by measuring ourselves can we identify areas of improvement. Such evaluations are meant to identify areas of strength and areas of growth. (see the evaluation chart at the end of this Appendix).

GAME PLAN

Personal Application not Theological Enquiry

It is important to recognize that the purpose of a men's group pursuing discipleship is primarily personal transformation rather than to acquire theological knowledge or understanding, although we will certainly grow in knowledge of God and understanding of his ways. The discipleship phase is not a period of extended theological investigation or intense biblical exegesis (interpretation). God, in his kindness, makes his plan for our life quite plain through a straightforward reading of Scripture and Church Teaching; the real work is that of implementation. Theological enquiry and advanced biblical exegesis are for a venue other than a men's group in a discipleship phase.

Application Exercise. Consider the passage from I Thessalonians 5.16-18:

> *Rejoice always, pray constantly, give thanks in all circumstances; for this is the will of God in Christ Jesus for you.*

Mark whether each of the following questions and statements relates to applying the passage to our life or to theological enquiry or advanced exegesis:

Life
App.

Theology/
Exegesis

_____ _____ How can we go about rejoicing even when I just got fired?

_____ _____ While I always thought prayer was a good idea, God's plan for me is to pray as much as I possibly can!

_____ _____ Does God the Father have a separate "will" from Jesus?

_____ _____ What habits or routines can I develop for rejoicing, interceding, and giving thanks throughout the day?

_____ _____ How much leisure time did first century residents of Thessalonica have? Given their presumed lower standard of living, were their circumstances more or less difficult than our own?

_____ _____ Is the Liturgy of the Hours a workable tool for me to implement this part of God's will for my life?

Why Women Live Longer than Men I
Step 1: Remove shoes
Step 2: Place metal ladder into water.
Step 3: Begin using POWER TOOLS while standing barefoot on the METAL LADDER in the WATER.

Universal Questions, Individual Applications

A men's group, particularly one in a discipleship phase, is a place of posing and discussing the questions related to implementing God's plan for our life: do we see ourselves as God does? how is our prayer life going? are we investing the right kind of time in our marriage? . . . Scripture and Tradition (including its many wise spiritual writers) help us identify the questions of discipleship. Some of these questions and challenges are developed in Part II of this book on Being a Disciple.

As disciples, we simply want to respond to the questions our Master poses to us and embrace the grace he offers for change. So a lot of what we do is ponder the questions of discipleship together, as well as the particular answers God has for our individual lives. In many cases, the question is pretty plain: for example, how am I going to spend time with God on a daily basis? Some will feel most comfortable with Scripture reading and meditation, while others prefer praying in a conversational manner or some other way. The important thing is that we face the questions God gives us in unfolding his plan for our lives, wrestle with them, determine what in particular God has for each of us in a given area, and then embrace his grace in changing our life accordingly.

One Size Doesn't Fit All

There is only one answer as to whether divorce is wrong: YES. However, there is no universal approach for a man trying to save his troubled marriage. Often, in grappling with how to live for God, one size doesn't fit all.

On questions of dogma and morality, the answers are almost always quite clear and conveniently spelled out in the *Catechism of the Catholic Church*. But for many aspects of transformation involved in discipleship, the answers – exactly what God has planned for us – vary from one person to the next. God gave us all unique families of origin, upbringings, personalities, gifts, capabilities, relationships, life experiences, educations, work experiences, family needs, privileges, and challenges, and, if we are married, a unique wife and unique children. As God transforms our lives, we retain our individuality, yet all come to resemble Jesus in terms of having a vibrant relationship with God, character, holiness, loving others, and living and praying for the kingdom. While all should have a pattern of life that supports and expresses our relationship with God, our transformation to be like Jesus and our active loving of who he loves, our pattern of life may look rather different from one man to the next.

Some will be able to pray an hour per day and have large amounts of discretionary time and money at their disposal. Others will have less time for prayer (though still a minimum amount each day) and discretionary resources due to demanding work lives, family responsibilities, chronic energy or pain diseases, deep emotional scares, etc. Some will come from families deeply rooted in the faith with parents who had the time and ability to closely pastor their kids. Others may hardly know one or both of their parents, have deep roots of bitterness, and lack a strong model from their family of God's love for them. Some will be single, others married or divorced. Some will be trying to establish their careers and have a large (or needy) family to care for, others will be much more thoroughly established in their work and have grown children.

Despite all our differences, every mature disciple will have an active relationship with God, will be undergoing transformation into Jesus' likeness and will be tangibly loving whom he loves.

Discussion Questions

Q1   Name some moral absolutes – commands that are always true regardless of the circumstances (e.g., taking innocent life):

> _____
> _____

Q2   What is the difference between a *moral absolute* and a *habit of discipleship* such as taking a daily prayer time?

_____
_____
_____

TEAMWORK

Success depends on team work and making plays. Teams that fail to work well together fail, a principle which is doubly true for men's groups pursuing discipleship where serving and praying for one another are the watchwords. And as in team sports, certain dynamics are necessary to make plays, the latter of which will be considered in the final section of this Appendix.

Maintain Zeal: Strive for the Prize

But as for you, man of God, shun all this; aim at righteousness, godliness, faith, love, steadfastness, gentleness. Fight the good fight of the faith; take hold of the eternal life to which you were called when you made the good confession in the presence of many witnesses.   I Timothy 6.11-12

Discipleship involves some "striving" on our part which the American Heritage Dictionary defines as:
1.   To exert much effort or energy; endeavor.
2.   To struggle or fight forcefully; contend: *strive against injustice.*

While it is God who transforms us, our efforts play an important role. We have to fight for it. In the words of St. Paul we press on, train, strive, struggle[51], run a race[52], fight the good fight[53] and even crucify one's flesh[54]. What does the struggle of gaining the prize of eternal life with God cost St. Paul, according to Philippians 3.8-14?

_____
_____
_____

What are some opposites of "striving"?
> _____
> _____
> _____

Strive as Peers

Most men's groups aren't led by a spiritual director, but by a facilitator. Even though some members of your group may seem more "transformed" than others or perhaps more gifted, all of us come together with various shortcomings and imperfections and need help in implementing God's plan in our lives (we are usually much more needy than we realize). So, unless our group has the good fortune of having a competent spiritual director, you're on the road of discipleship together as peers, through which God can work quite powerfully!

Why Women Live Longer than Men II
Necessity is the mother of invention

Love and Pray for One Another

We have not ceased to pray for you, asking that you may be filled with the knowledge of his will in all spiritual wisdom and understanding, to lead a life worthy of the Lord, fully pleasing to him, bearing fruit in every good work and increasing in the knowledge of God. May you be strengthened with all power, according to his glorious might, for all endurance and patience with joy.

Colossians 1.9-11

Disciples pray for one another, which both helps others grow and increases our love for them. The *agape* love that Jesus talks about is one of practical service to one another. God wants us to strive together towards the goals of discipleship. The New Testament speaks directly to this need to work together:

Let us consider how to stir up one another to love and good works, not neglecting to meet together, as is the habit of some, but encouraging one another.

Hebrews 10:24-25

Therefore encourage one another and build one another up, just as you are doing. I Thessalonians 5:11

Put on then, as God's chosen ones, holy and beloved, compassion, kindness, lowliness, meekness, and patience, . . . above all these put on love . . . teach and admonish one another in all wisdom. Col 3.12-16

Brethren, if a man is overtaken in any trespass, you who are spiritual should restore him in a spirit of gentleness. Galatians 6.1

List the six commands in these passages regarding helping one another be disciples:

1) _____
2) _____
3) _____
4) _____
5) _____
6) _____

How can your men's group serve to "encourage one another and build one another up"?

_____
_____
_____

How can your men's group "stir one another up to love and good works"?

_____
_____
_____

MAKING PLAYS

Candor, Commitment & Confidentiality

> Let each of you <u>look not only to his own interests, but also to the interests of others</u>. Have this mind among yourselves, which is yours in Christ Jesus (who died to save and transform us)   Philippians 2.4-11

We learn at a young age what happens when we fail to watch out for our self – somebody pulls the chair out from under us! The school of hard knocks teaches us to guard our weaknesses and to cloak our vulnerabilities. However, in the spiritual life candor is indispensable to God changing us. In particular, one must freely:

- identify problems and weaknesses
- admit sins and shortcomings
- welcome encouragement and suggestions for improvement

The old saying is to not throw our pearls before swine. Nor should we turn our backside to a charging bull – which is what you'll do by opening up to uncommitted men. Unless each of the men in the group is really committed to assisting each other toward the common goals of becoming like Christ and loving who he loves, find a group that is.

159

As well, confidentiality is absolutely necessary for men to freely share their struggles and challenges with one another. Only a fool makes himself vulnerable to blabbermouths but a wise man reveals his weaknesses to trustworthy friends. Anyone who violates confidentiality except for grave reasons (e.g., to avert serious harm to someone) should be strongly rebuked if not expelled from the group.

Accountability

Iron sharpens iron, and one man sharpens another.

Proverbs 27.17

Why Women Live Longer than Men III
I'm sure this guy still wonders WHY he got fired!

New Years resolutions are quickly forgotten. An excellent way to boost our success in reaching our discipleship goals is to make our self accountable. In high school football you make yourself accountable to the coach to make the practices and to work hard. The football coach challenges and pushes you to be successful, offering praise and encouragement. You are ashamed to run wind sprints weakly.

Consider making yourself accountable to your men's group for some of your discipleship goals. Encourage each other. Challenge each other. Of course, making our self accountable to each other is simply harnessing a natural force among men. Men don't like to fail. Having to admit failure to the guys in our group can be a powerful incentive to hit our goals. While accountability may help us to get in the habit of praying, never lose sight of the real reason for prayer: simply being with God.

Spiritual Goal Setting

This was covered in Part I, Lesson 6.

Safeguard Personal Autonomy

If our men's group could make discipleship choices for us, cows would be in Heaven! God gives us freedom to embrace or reject what is good, unlike barnyard animals. Our men's group can't embrace God's plan for our life – *only we can*. They can encourage and challenge us – but never make decisions for us. God made us free beings capable of rejoicing in, and choosing for, his goodness, truth and beauty rather than as insensible cows capable only of being prodded into his presence.

In working together in implementing God's plan for our lives, we must respect each others personal autonomy and relate to one another peer-to-peer, brother–to-brother. Helping a person see clearly a particular question that the Master poses to him as a disciple or discuss together a particular area of transformation is desirable. But persuading, even gently, an individual to follow the response you think is appropriate for him may undermine his autonomy (again, we are concerned here with areas of growth and transformation, not sin, against which we should be rather persuasive).

Indeed, A person must freely choose God's plan for themselves. Hopefully, we are open to hearing how others view how God's plan applies to one's life and to freely discussing the challenges one faces, but the responsibility is ours alone to make the choice for any aspect of our life.

Men will indeed make bad choices. Nevertheless, the men's group, including its facilitator, must limit itself to discussing and offering advice. Each member of the group must firmly make decisions for himself and avoid any semblance of governing their life "by committee". A person having difficulty making decisions for himself should consider leaving a men's group pursuing discipleship. We can implement God's plan for our life only by freely embracing it.

Tackling Deep-seated Problems

Some problems that we face, or encountered earlier in life, inflict emotional and psychological scars that often require help beyond that of a men's discipleship group. Some patterns of sin are so addictive and so diminish our wills – ranging from substance abuse to pornography - that outside help is also usually required. The reality is that with each passing year our culture more and more fiercely assaults almost every aspect of God's plan for our lives, leaving a wake of misery and destruction rather than happiness and joy. While a men's discipleship group is the right spiritual base for fighting such inherently spiritual problems, increasingly, men will need supplemental help outside the men's group. Such help can come from qualified psychologists; marital counselors; and programs for breaking sex and substance addictions, such as AA and other Twelve Step programs. Please see the NFCM and GodsPlanforYourLife.org websites for a listing of some of

> **A Trail of Wreckage**
>
> The consequences of sin – your own or those near you - are not very pretty. Something like half of those counting themselves Christian men in the U.S. have serious pornography, masturbation or other sexual addictions. Many have serious emotional scarring from parents who divorced or from having been abused at one point or another during one's life. Sexual intercourse outside of marriage and broken relationships may have seriously undermined your ability to trust your spouse or to view her as little more than a sexual object. The intense pre-occupation of our society with performing physically, academically or professionally may leave you with a deeply flawed self image. Or craving love and attention from fellow human beings who are themselves increasingly self-absorbed perhaps has contributed to some eating disorders. Same-sex attractions are also more likely today in a society of many disordered families and one that elevates sexual fulfillment above almost all else.

these programs. The group should be supportive and encouraging to a member grappling with a deep-seated problem as long as he is fully committed to change. Yet, however challenging one man's problem, it should not come to dominate the group's discussion.

Finish Strong

I have fought the good fight, I have finished the race, I have kept the faith

II Timothy 4.7

Another important dynamic is that discipleship is a life long process. This was true for the Apostle Paul and it's true for us! While we can enter into and maintain a relationship with God, the relationship can always be deepened, at least this side of heaven. In fact, we will find that God consistently challenges us to go deeper, to trust him more, to simply have more of him and be more fully his.

While God can significantly transform some major aspects of our life if we really give ourselves over to his plan, there is always room for further growth in becoming like Jesus. He wants us to be perfect even as he himself is perfect! Our transformation finds completion only upon our entrance into his heavenly courts with resurrected bodies. While we can love who God loves, the purity of our love for others is tied to the degree to which God transforms us. And the intensity and joy of loving others peaks only when we are fully transformed into his likeness, again, upon our entrance into heaven.

I hope your expectations are sufficiently high for what God plans for us! In a relatively short period of time, you can expect tremendous joy from being with him and loving what he loves and much amazing transformation into being like him by really devoting our self to following him. Yet, there's more, so much more, that God plans for us for the rest of our life, indeed, for all eternity.

On the other hand, we must keep in mind that just as sin (our own and that of others towards us) damages us and has a tendency to *negatively transform* us, it may take an excruciating long period of time for God to transform certain areas of our life. As a child I used to have fits of rage, which were in part a response to being bullied by others. Today I still struggle with staying cool when my computer crashes or with even slighter provocations! According to no less authority than my wife, while God has increased my patience greatly over our years of marriage, yes, there remains plenty of room for improvement.

Discussion Questions

Q1 - If you had a sex addiction problem, would you be willing to share about your struggles with the other men in your group? Why or why not?

_____

_____

Q2 - What are the dangers of "positive peer pressure"?

_____

_____

_____

Q3 - Do you struggle with "looking good"? In what ways can trying to look good be an impediment to spiritual growth?

_____

_____

_____

EVALUATION MATRIX

Area	Dynamic	Rate Yourself
Basics Skills	Attendance, prep and enthusiasm	
	Maintain group focus	
	Balanced participation by all group members	
Team Captain	Servant Leadership	
	Facilitator Duties	
Game Plan	Focus on personal application, not theological enquiry	
	Pose universal questions; Seek individual answers	
	Recognize that "one size doesn't fit all" in terms of personal prayer time, use of our time, individual gifting, etc.	
Teamwork	Zeal for pursuing God's plan for our lives	
	Strive together as peers	
	Love and pray for one another	
Making Plays	Make group a "safe place" to share about our goals, challenges, failures, and successes	
	Role of goal setting and accountability	
	Safeguard of personal autonomy in decision making	
	Tackling deep-seated problems & finishing strong	

Appendix: Examination of Conscience
(daily devotional use)

The Two Greatest Commandments

I. You shall love the Lord your God with all your heart, with all your mind and with all your soul.

Have I fully embraced God's plan for my life? Have I allowed Jesus to be **Lord** of my life by actively seeking grace to grow in holiness and love? Did I fail to pray daily? Have I lived in **Faith** and trust in God? Am I living in **Hope** of heaven by how I use my resources and time? Do I express my **Love** for God by loving my neighbor?

II. You shall love your neighbor as yourself.

Was I cheerful and caring towards my family and those I have responsibility for? In the chance encounter with a neighbor? Have I **interceded** for those who don't know Christ? Was I humble, kind, generous, chaste, and patient with others? Have I loved my neighbor through **Corporal Works of Mercy:** feed the hungry, give drink to the thirsty, clothe the naked, visit the imprisoned, shelter the homeless, visit the sick and bury the dead? Have I loved my neighbor through **Spiritual Works of Mercy:** admonish the sinner, instruct the ignorant, counsel the doubtful, comfort the sorrowful, bear wrongs patiently, forgive all injuries and pray for the living and the dead? Was I uncharitable in word or deed? Did I give bad example, fight or quarrel? Did I neglect my duties to my husband, wife, children or parents? Was I impatient, angry, envious, unkind, proud, jealous, revengeful, hateful toward others or lazy? Did I gossip or reveal the faults and sins of others? Did I fail to keep secrets that I should have kept? Have I **cooperated** in another's sin by counsel, command, consent, provocation, praise, concealment, partaking, silence, or defense?

Growth in Holiness and Charity

The Theological Virtues
Faith, Hope and Charity.

The Cardinal Virtues
Prudence, Justice, Temperance and Fortitude.

Gifts of the Holy Spirit (Isaiah 11)
Wisdom, Understanding, Counsel, Might, Knowledge, and Fear of the Lord.

The Fruits of the Holy Spirit (Galatians 5)
Love, joy, peace, patience, kindness, goodness, faithfulness, gentleness and self-control.

The Beatitudes (Matthew 5)
I. Blessed are the poor in spirit;
   for theirs is the Kingdom of Heaven.
2. Blessed are they that mourn;
   for they shall be comforted.
3. Blessed are the meek;
   for they shall possess the land.
4. Blessed are they that hunger and thirst
   for justice; for they shall be filled.

Works of the Flesh (Galatians 5)
Fornication, impurity, licentiousness, idolatry, sorcery, enmity, strife, jealousy, anger, selfishness, dissension, party spirit, envy, drunkenness, carousing, and the like.

The Seven Capital Sins and their opposite Virtues
1. Pride - Humility.
2. Avarice - Generosity.
3. Lust - Chastity.
4. Anger - Meekness.
5. Gluttony - Temperance.
6. Envy - Brotherly Love.
7. Sloth or Acadia - Diligence.

5. Blessed are the merciful;
   for they shall obtain mercy.
6. Blessed are the pure of heart;
   for they shall see God.
7. Blessed are the peacemakers;
   for they shall be called the children of God.
8. Blessed are they that suffer persecution for
   righteousness' sake;
   for theirs is the Kingdom of Heaven.

Sins Against the Holy Spirit

1. Presumption on God's Mercy.
2. Despair.
3. Resisting and/or Attacking the known truth.
4. Envy at another's spiritual good.
5. Obstinacy in sin.
6. Final impenitence.

The Ten Commandments

I. I am the Lord Thy God. Thou shall not have strange gods before Me.
- Did I believe in horoscopes, fortune telling, dreams, good luck charms or reincarnation?
- Did I despair of or presume on God's mercy?

II. Thou shall not take the Name of the Lord thy God in vain.
- Did I blaspheme God or take God's Name in vain, curse or break an oath or vow?
- Did I go to Holy Communion in the state of mortal sin?

III. Remember to keep holy the Lord's Day.
- Did I miss Mass on a Sunday or a Holy Day of Obligation? Was I inattentive at Mass, arrive late or leave early?
- Did I do unnecessary work on Sunday?

IV. Honor thy father and thy mother.
- Did I disobey or disrespect my parents or legitimate superiors? Have I cared for my parents?

V. Thou shall not kill.
- Did I physically injure anyone? Did I abuse drugs or alcohol?
- Have I advised anyone to have an abortion? Did I vote to protect the unborn?

VI. Thou shall not commit adultery.
- Was I faithful to my marriage vows? Have I kept company with another's spouse?

VII. Thou shall not steal.
Did I give a full day's work in return for a full day's pay? Did I give a fair wage to my employee(s)?
Did I fulfill my contracts, give or accept bribes, or pay my bills? Did I steal, cheat, help or encourage others to steal or keep stolen goods? Did I rashly gamble or speculate or deprive my family of the necessities of life? Did I cheat on my taxes?

VIII. Thou shall not bear false witness.
- Did I tell lies deliberately in order to deceive or injure others or to benefit myself?

IX. Thou shall not covet thy neighbor's wife.
Did I dress immodestly? Did I use impure or suggestive words? Did I tell, or listen to, impure stories? Did I willfully entertain impure thoughts and desires? Did I deliberately look at impure television, internet, plays, pictures or movies or read impure material? Did I perform impure acts by myself (masturbation) or with another?

X. Thou shall not covet thy neighbor's goods.
Have I been materialistic? Am I pre-occupied with acquiring things?

Obedience to Church Law: "what [the apostles] bind on earth is bound in heaven," Matthew 16.19

Have I failed to educate myself concerning the teachings of the Church? Did I fail to contribute to the support of the Church? Did I go to Holy Communion without fasting for one hour or more from food and drink (water and medicine are permitted)? Did I practice artificial birth control or was I permanently sterilized (tubal ligation or vasectomy)?

End Notes

[1] Paragraphs 57 and 60.

[2] *Our Hearts Were Burning within Us: A Pastoral Plan for Adult Faith Formation in the United States*, U.S. Bishops, 1999.

[3] CCC 2813.

[4] Purity of heart also concerns charity and love of truth and orthodoxy of faith (CCC 2518).

[5] Above all, prayer involves "a vital and personal relationship with the living and true God" (CCC 2558); and "the life of prayer is the habit of being in the presence of the thrice-holy God and in communion with him" (CCC 2565). Of course, the Mass is the pre-eminent prayer of the Church. These lessons, however, are primarily concerned with personal prayer rather than corporate worship. The excellent discussion of prayer in the *Catechism of the Catholic Church* identifies several categories of prayer that I have implicitly grouped under Contemplation: Blessing and Adoration and Praise. Transformational prayer, as discussed above, as well as seeking God's particular guidance for our life can both be considered aspects of intercessory prayer. Again, this whole lesson is worthy of a more extended practical treatment which is planned as another title in this series. Of course, much more can be said about Scripture reading, study and memorization. See www.GodsPlanForYourLife.org for a resource listing and links.

[6] *Novo Millenio Ineunte* 33. Contemplation is used a bit more broadly in this lesson and includes aspects of praise and adoration.

[7] One might say that this lesson is about "basic contemplation" and speaks especially of aids to contemplation. It is important to remember that true contemplation is a gift from God. However, there are many things we can do to prepare ourselves to receive this gift.

[8] See II Corinthians 4.6 *inter alia*. Due to its limited scope this study primarily considers God's beauty; in a sense, to the extent God's other attributes are attractive we consider them beautiful. Glory, *kabod* in Hebrew and *doxa* in Greek, has a parallel though somewhat different connotation than beauty and also captures some of the overall character of God. Philosophically, the word *sublime* is often used to mean something akin to spiritual beauty. See pages 15-28 of David Hart's *The Beauty of the Infinite* (Grand Rapids/Cambridge: Eerdmans, 2003) for a rigorous discussion of how to define beauty. You may also consult pages 34-45 (and beyond) of von Balthasar's magisterial *The Glory of the Lord: A Theological Aesthetic, Vol. I, Seeing the Form* tr. by Leiva-Merikakis, Fessio and Riches (San Francisco: Ignatius, 1982).

[9] This question may be a bit of a stumper for many since we are often too caught up in our everyday lives to notice beauty – just put down anything that comes to mind and revisit this question after reading through the rest of the lesson.

[10] Holiness simply describes God as being utterly different or apart. One synonym is being "godlike" or "godly." In a certain way, the perfection of all of God's other attributes make up his holiness.

[11] A simple listing of God's titles may be found online at: http://www.jesuswalk.com/ebooks/pu_names-god_list.htm.

[12] Cf. *Novo Millennio Ineunte* 32-33, which describes our conversation with Christ as being "wrought by the Holy Spirit" and eventually renders us persons "vibrating at the Spirit's touch."

[13] . . . and on a bad day? Give thanks anyway! The reality of prayer is that we will always be fighting distractions of many types. Press on despite your headaches. Over time, our battle with distractions diminishes.

[14] Romans 8.26-27; Matthew 6.10; CCC 2610-11.

[15] I Peter 2.5, CCC 1546-7. Cf. CCC 901-3.

[16] Matthew 6.25-33; 7.7-11.

[17] Matthew 6.7.

[18] CCC 2673-79; 2708.

[19] See the section on Personality and Piety, pages 45-73, in *Invitation to a Journey* by M. Robert Mulholland, Jr. (Intervarsity: Downers Grove, 1993).

[20] CCC 2664.

[21] CCC 2653.

[22] cf. CCC 1174-78; 2585-89.

[23] Cf. CCC 2705-8.

[24] And every day, if possible. Both going to daily Mass and taking a prayer or Scripture time (like the Holy Father) may be the ideal, but we live in the real world of time constraints, schedules and logistics. Of course, you have to decide the best mix for yourself. On the one hand, the Church emphasizes the importance of personal prayer and Scripture reading by devoting one of the four sections of its *Catechism* to prayer. On the other hand, the Church holds up the Eucharist as the source and summit of your faith.

[25] "Flesh" is translated in the Jerusalem Bible as "unspiritual"; see the brilliant analysis of the usage of flesh in the extensive note to Romans 7.5 in the Jerusalem Bible.

[26] See *Made to Be Like Him* (forthcoming).

[27] CCC 734 and 1972, respectively.

[28] CCC 2003. Grace has other important dimensions including justification. See CCC 1996-2029. This study will refer to grace primarily in terms of God's power and simply as (the work of) the Holy Spirit.

[29] See Matthew 6.16-18 and CCC 2549.

[30] *The American Heritage® Dictionary of the English Language*, Fourth Edition, downloaded from Dictionary.com on June 11, 2005.

[31] Although, somewhat paradoxically, such effort on our part is itself only possible because God so inclines us, CCC 2001.

[32] Luke 13.24, Luke 12.51-53, Luke 14.28-31, and Matthew 5.29-30.

[33] E.g., Galatians 5.13, 24; Ephesians 6.10-17.

[34] Cf. the terminology of Colossians 3: "putting to death what is earthly in us" and "putting on our new nature."

[35] Many important things are touched on here, such as conscience, contrition, and mortal sin, which warrant further development, such as can be found in the Catechism. *Made to be Like Him* also provides a more extensive treatment of these concepts.

[36] Here again, I note the inadequacies of space and refer you to the planned companion to this book, *Made to Be Like Him*; check www.GodsPlanforYourLife.org for further details, and in the mean time, consult the Life in Christ section of the CCC, 1691-2557 and your local Catholic bookstore. You will find a decent amount of material in the CCC by simply checking the topical index at the back of the book.

[37] Matthew 5.17-20, which, as we have seen, drives us to God himself on a daily – if not hourly - basis, in order to gain the power to do so: his Holy Spirit. The *Catechism of the Catholic Church* systematically lays out the Lord's teaching on morality in 2052 to 2558, following the order implied by the Ten Commandments.

[38] Ibid.

[39] Galatians 5.22-23.

[40] Persons lacking an explicit relationship with God in Christ may implicitly although imperfectly embrace God's plan by following their consciences, loving and caring for others, working and building good things – all of which please God.

[41] Again, a more extensive treatment of these topics may be found in, *Made to be Like Him*; check www.GodsPlanforYourLife.org for availability of this study.

[42] See, for example, John 13-15.

43 CCC 2500.

44 "What! This author is nuts!" Yeah, I know you are probably busy and stressed out over lack of time with your loved ones and stretching to make the next mortgage payment. That's why I saved this nugget till the end of the study. Nonetheless, objectively, Americans consume something like five to ten times more than the average person on the planet. Each of us will have to answer for what we do with the resources that are obviously way more than is necessary for basic life. Let Matthew 7.13-14 and Matthew 25 be your guides, together with the countless saints the Church holds up as examples. We can't outdo God in generosity: see Matthew 19.16-30.

45 *On Catechesis in our Time*, paragraph 61.

46 I Peter 3.15, CCC 900, 905.

47 See CCC 767-768. Some Catholics experience an even more profound outpouring of God's Holy Spirit – see the Charismatic Renewal; these gifts are available to those who earnestly ask Jesus for them.

48 *Our Hearts Were Burning within Us: A Pastoral Plan for Adult Faith Formation in the United States*, U.S. Bishops, 1999, paragraph 45.

49 Some readers will complain that the *Catechism's* description is somewhat ponderous! I can refer the reader to my book, *Made for Joy*, Lessons I-III, that provides a more readable and approachable consideration of God's saving love for us in Jesus and through the Holy Spirit.

50 Facilitators may also find profit in reviewing the section on "leading healthy discussions".

51 I Tim 4.7-9.

52 I Corinthians 9:24; II Timothy 4:7.

53 I Timothy 6.12; II Timothy 4.7.

54 Galatians 5.24.

CPSIA information can be obtained at www.ICGtesting.com
Printed in the USA
BVOW060128310712

296634BV00003B/1/A